I HATE
MY BOSS!

D0626988

Also by Bob Weinstein:

Who Says There Are No Jobs Out There? 25 Irreverent Rules for Getting a Job

"So What If I'm 50?": Straight Talk and Proven Strategies for Getting Hired in the Toughest Job Market Ever

Résumés Don't Get Jobs: The Realities and Myths of Job Hunting

I HATE MY BOSS!

How to Survive
and Get Ahead
When Your Boss
Is a Tyrant,
Control Freak, or
Just Plain Nuts!

BOB WEINSTEIN

McGraw-Hill
New York   San Francisco   Washington, D.C.   Auckland   Bogotá
Caracas   Lisbon   London   Madrid   Mexico City   Milan
Montreal   New Delhi   San Juan   Singapore
Sydney   Tokyo   Toronto

Library of Congress Cataloging-in-Publication Data applied for.

McGraw-Hill

A Division of The McGraw·Hill Companies

1 2 3 4 5 6 7 8 9 0   DOC/DOC   9 0 2 1 0 9 8 7

ISBN 0-07-069194-0

The sponsoring editor for this book was Betsy Brown, the editing supervisor was Patricia V. Amoroso, and the production supervisor was Pamela Pelton. It was set in Fairfield by Terry Leaden of McGraw-Hill's Professional Book Group composition unit.

Printed and bound by R. R. Donnelley & Sons Company.

This publication is designed to provide accurate and authoritative information in regard to the subject matter covered. It is sold with the understanding that the publisher is not engaged in rendering legal, accounting, or other professional service. If legal advice or other expert assitance is required, the services of a competent professional person should be sought.
 —*From a declaration of principles jointly adopted by a committee of the American Bar Association and a committee of publishers.*

This book is printed on recycled, acid-free paper containing a minimum of 50% recycled de-inked fiber.

For Bonnie

CONTENTS

INTRODUCTION:
SO YOU HATE YOUR BOSS!
WHAT ELSE IS NEW?

As soon as you have one person (a boss) telling another person (an employee) what to do, problems are inevitable. And the problems stem from both sides of the equation: from the person giving the orders and the person taking them. That fundamental truth will never change.

If Adam answered to a boss—as he probably did from Eden—chances are he would have had problems too. Why should he be any different?

The complex boss-worker relationship has always been fraught with problems. The reasons include everything from unpredictable human chemistry to the fear and abhorrence many of us have with authority. Whether your boss seems like Adolf Hitler or the Maharishi, many of us have a problem taking orders. And still others who crave having someone tell them what to do are cursed with demonic bosses. Unfair, you rant. Whoever said it's a just world?

Despite the complexities of modern living, there aren't too many people one has to get along with in life. Casting aside misanthropic loners, most people rank family and friends high on the list. But unless you're born wealthy, you must get along with the bosses in your life. They're the ones who feed, clothe, and support your lifestyle.

Make no mistake about it. All companies, whether small or multinational, are political hotbeds. Success within an organization is contingent upon forging a positive relationship with your boss. How well you do so dictates your organizational fate. If you respect the power structure and gain the accompanying support of your boss, the doors leading to the golden corridors of opportunity will spring open.

The organizational fast-trackers in the world are people-persons and team players. Uppermost, they're political animals who respect and understand the pecking order. They're the ones most likely to build healthy relationships with their bosses. Besides reorganizations, downsizings, and reasons beyond our control, most people get fired because they can't get on with their boss. On performance appraisal forms, that comes under the organizational-speak heading of "interpersonal issues." These are the people who hate their boss. In return, the boss hates them. Mutual distrust is the foundation of the relationship. But those who work at building tight relationships based on respect and need are the most secure. If a downsizing takes place, they're most likely to hold onto their jobs or are among the last to go.

No matter how smart, enlightened, brilliant, or neurotic you are, unless you chuck it all and move to Tibet or a deserted island, problem bosses are unavoidable. The $64,000 question is: What do you do when you have a boss from hell? Quit? Throw yourself on the floor and have a screaming, arm-thrashing temper tantrum? Take a contract out on his or her life? Sorry, none of those solutions will do much good. However, developing a strategy that not only helps you cope but also thrive with a difficult boss ought to be your goal. That's what you're going to learn in the pages ahead. Stick around. I guarantee you'll be able to pick your boss out of the lineup.

ACKNOWLEDGMENTS

This book wouldn't have happened if it weren't for all the brutal bosses I had to endure over a turbulent career. But I wasn't alone. There were hundreds of others who had far worse experiences. Most of them—thank God—are still alive to talk about them. I'd like to thank all the people who told me confidential horror stories about bosses they survived. If it weren't for all the courageous people who agreed to speak with me, this book couldn't have been written. I'd also like to thank my buddy and colleague Tom Popp for helping me weld a tight manuscript; my wife for enduring an off-the-wall journalist trying to juggle too many projects at once; my mom for having me; my dad for introducing me to Beethoven's *Ninth* when I was three; my daughter Jenny for tirelessly working the phones around-the-clock tracking people who had miserable boss experiences; my son Josh for spending six months staking out and recording his impressions of psychotic boss behavior; my son-in-law Enrique "Titti" Ball for tirelessly looting newsstands and libraries and evading local police in eight states in pursuit of demented boss material; Frank "Frankie" Dobisky and Jim Crismon at Dobisky Associates and John McGauley at Gehring Associates for providing some excellent sources; my dog Archie for driving me home countless times when I was too tired to take the wheel; and my high school buddy Lem "Tiny Tim" Brodsky for keeping my creative engine fueled with top-of the-line single malt scotch. And last but not least, the good Lord, for watching over me and taking care of the ones I love.

Bob Weinstein

I HATE
MY BOSS!

GRIN AND BEAR IT!

You Can't Pick Your Kids— or Your Boss

Humorist Gene Perret has some pithy one-liners about hard-nosed bosses that are bound to hit home:

- "This man has a black belt in management."
- "He's like 'Dirty Harry' with an M.B.A."
- "He has an M.B.A. after his name. That's because he's a member of Mean Bastards Anonymous."
- "His goal in life is to someday own and operate a Turkish prison."

Let's lay out a few givens so we can deal honestly with this nasty person we call our "boss." There are a raft of things we can control in our lives. We can pick our friends, spouses, careers, and the place we live. But we can't pick our kids or our bosses. If we're lucky, we will be blessed with decent low-maintenance kids who don't wind up in jail. Yet, some parents have no choice but to make the best of loathsome offspring.

Bosses are another story. You can pick your job and the type of company you'd like to work for, but you can't pick the boss for whom you'll work. It would be great if you could, but few of us can afford to spin on our heels when we meet a boss who acts like the incarnation of Satan. Yet, most of us have a sixth sense about hellish bosses. Without even trying, this person broadcasts nasty vibes. The only things missing are red

1

fiery eyes, fangs, and slime oozing from his or her mouth and nose. How you handle this discovery will determine whether you'll make a healthy adjustment or give yourself an ulcer.

DON'T BE SO SENSITIVE, IT'S NOT YOUR FAULT. AND NO, YOU'RE NOT BEING PUNISHED

Most of us start jobs with the wrong attitude. No sooner do we sense that there are horns protruding from our boss's head than we set ourselves up for a long journey through hell. "I don't know how I'm going to schlep in here every morning and work with that lunatic. I haven't worked here for a week yet and I'm already thinking about whacking her." Or you toss in a little self-blame and say to yourself, "Why me? I must have done something really bad in a past life to deserve this two-legged monster." Or, "Other people get decent bosses. Why can't I get a break for once?" If feeling sorry for ourselves yields temporary relief, we'll try that as well. In fact, we'll make ourselves believe anything that will help us deal with the torture ahead.

But these self-defeating techniques achieve nothing; they only help us to avoid the obvious task ahead of getting along with this person. Rather than avoiding the issue, let's confront it head-on by digesting three tips that set the stage for a har-monious working relationship with your boss.

"I'M GOING TO GET ALONG WITH THIS PERSON IF IT KILLS ME"

THREE TIPS FOR BUILDING A POSITIVE ATTITUDE

1. *Accept that you have no options.*   Knowing that simple truth should get you off to a good start. Most people work so they can pay their bills, feed and clothe themselves, and if

there is anything left, have some fun in the bargain. Of course you should love what you do, but for most people, working is primarily a practical pursuit. So, even if your boss stalks the hall armed with a bullwhip, a chain, and a sawed-off shotgun, you're not about to quit because you don't like this person.

2. *Do what most people do: Tough it out.* Rather than just stick it out, why not fine-tune your attitude and try to make the best of it? Come to terms with a simple reality: You need your employer more than he or she needs you. How's that for putting it on the line? Everyone is replaceable, but you're more replaceable than your boss is. These realities set the stage for adopting an attitude that will lay the foundation for success rather than failure.

3. *Depersonalize the relationship.* It's human nature to take things personally. A built-in narcissism thrusts us center stage in many situations involving others. We make ourselves the focus when in fact we're only a by-product of an event. Countless times we blame emotionally charged situations with bosses on ourselves, even when we're not the cause of the problem. Perhaps it's our own grandiosity tied to unrealistic feelings of self-importance, but we give ourselves a starring role when we're only a bit player in a larger drama. Rarely do we consider that our boss is reacting to pressure from above that has nothing to do with us. Organizations are chains of command with all bosses kowtowing to their superiors. The larger the organization, the more complicated the pecking order. Even CEOs have bosses. If they displease stockholders, they're given the heave-ho. Of course, they're a lot more secure than you and I, but it proves that they also have problems from above.

Bosses, whether low-level supervisors or high-ranking executives, often take their frustrations, pent-up anxiety, and rage out on subordinates. That's you and I. Unless they start flinging bodies out windows, there are seldom repercussions. Unfair? You bet it is, but who said business is fair? Nonetheless, it doesn't have to be that way. If your boss is being pressured by his boss, chances are he'll start breathing down your neck, mainly to make himself feel better. Do you expect him to tell off his boss and risk souring the relationship, getting fired, or jeopardizing his chances of moving up? That's the divine organizational pecking order. Every boss needs a safe scapegoat. Your goal is not to become your boss's whipping person.

Get the picture? Look at organizations as a microcosm of society—unpredictable, political, and fraught with hidden conflicts and agendas. Consider the relationship with your boss from a practical standpoint. It shouldn't be based on thinking, "If this birdbrain says one more nasty thing, I'm going to kill him," but rather, "I'm not going to let this person stand in the way of building my career. I'm going to make the most of the situation." Achieving that attitude is easier said than done, but it's worth trying.

Advice: Remember why you're working. You need the job to keep body and soul together, but you're also building a career. The job is only a steppingstone. You're not going to be there forever. Do it well, build solid contacts, and get a good recommendation from your boss, and you'll either move up in the same organization or leave for a better job. Mess up the relationship with your boss, and your career prospects at that company will suffer. You may not be fired, but you'll wallow in limbo and go nowhere.

Just as you sensed negative vibes about your boss the moment you met, don't think your boss hasn't picked up your hate waves as well. The boss may not say anything, but he or she knows that they're there. Your negative attitude is sure to sentence you to indentured servitude under his or her command. Unless you quit for a better job, you're hopelessly stuck. *Advice:* Take a constructive path and work at building a solid working relationship with your boss.

4. *Realize that perfect jobs and perfect bosses are myths.* Get real. How many people do you know that hold a perfect job? This includes everything from an ideal work setting and organizational culture to cooperative bosses and peers. It's a workingperson's Nirvana, a corporate Valhalla, without greed and backstabbing. Show me that such an organization exists, and I'll refund the money you spent on this book. But that will never happen because a perfect job is only a fantasy. Even the smallest organizations are rife with politics. As soon as you have two or more people reporting to one boss, you have politics. That means at least two underlings are jockeying for power and competing for the boss's attention. Multiply that by 100 or 1000 and you have an accurate picture of organizational life. The more players in the organizational labyrinth, the greater the chances of skulduggery in the ranks. It makes for a less than perfect situation.

Competition is healthy, but when it gets out of hand, it breeds greed and infighting within the corporate ranks. *Advice:* Idealism is fine up to a point. But view the world as it is, not as you'd like it to be. Human beings are flawed, imperfect creatures. Aristotle hit the proverbial nail on the head when he said, "Man is by nature a political animal." That includes you. Don't waste time searching for perfect jobs or companies. They're only mirages within your own mind.

PLAY THE GAME

This practical advice is designed to help you start out on the right foot with your boss. If you can accomplish that, you've got a strong toehold on your future. In the critical building stage of your relationship, coexistence is the name of the game. You don't have to be best buddies nor should you bend over backwards to make a great impression. You simply have to get along with this person.

Advice: The importance of the early stages of the relationship cannot be emphasized enough. This is when you size up each other, read each other's rhythms, and find out what makes each other tick. You'll have a better idea how to control the situation once you understand where your boss is coming from. Do that well and you're on your way to mastering the organizational game. In the final analysis, it is a game. Getting a job is the initial stage of the game. Keeping it is the second part, and the third and most important part is succeeding. You're not going to achieve that step if you don't hit it off with your boss. The way to do so is by thoroughly understanding the dynamics of the relationship.

IT'S ONLY A JOB

My mom used to give me some advice when I was bent out of shape about something, saying, "It's not worth getting sick over." I never thought I'd be agreeing with her, but the wise woman was dead on the money. While it's human nature to take everything personally, you must fight that mechanism and separate yourself from your job. This can only be achieved through cool, reflective, and objective moments. That's when you see the world as it is and realize that most jobs are only brief chapters in our lives. Statistics say you'll hold a job between 2 and 5 years. That's not a long time, especially when you consider it only occupies 35 to 40 hours a week. *Remember:* You are released from work at the end of the shift 5 days a week. A job only *feels* like a prison. Your boss is not really your warden. He or she is only a temporary official in your life. You're free to leave whenever you like.

Ponder these realities. We'll be stressing them throughout the book. Let's find out why it's so easy to hate your boss.

IT'S EASY TO HATE YOUR BOSS

He watches Jacques Cousteau specials and roots for the sharks.

GENE PERRET

Funny Business, Prentice Hall

Bosses are custom-made, factory-approved objects of hatred. They remind me of those inflatable clowns I bought for my kids so they could unleash their hostility by punching them all over the house. If Freud were alive today, he'd have a field day raking in big bucks as an organizational consultant, running around the country to consult with employers on problem employees.

There are certain unsaid, unwritten rules by which we all live. Call them laws of nature—unofficial commandments handed down from the big guy above. In fact, they're so ingrained in our psyche that we're not even aware of them. They say we can't hate our folks or family, especially our moms, wives, or kids. But everyone else is fair game. Bosses are by far the best of the lot. They're even better than mothers-in-law.

Think of bosses as surrogate parents. Although many of us have a problem with that kind of relationship, it often has nothing to do with our boss. We put up with taking orders from our folks, but we have a problem with others such as teachers, especially cantankerous disciplinarians who act out their dictator fantasies in class. Many of us endured military service, which is all about chain of command, taking orders, and being obedient. Then, once we become mature adults ready to make a place for ourselves in the world, we find that we still have to take orders. This time, they're from our bosses.

We resent it because we think we're stuck in a subservient role, doomed to spend the rest of our lives butt-kissing people we detest. No one prepared us for such a cruel fate. It's even worse when we're forced to take orders from someone who is 10 or 15 years our junior. "I can't believe I have to take orders from this punk kid who just started shaving."

Some of us have a problem taking orders from bosses of the opposite sex. Men are more likely to have a problem with female bosses, whereas many women report they'd prefer to work for a man. It's hard to believe, but even in these emancipated times, plenty of macho guys insist women belong at home cooking, breeding, and cleaning.

A RELATIONSHIP BUILT ON RESENTMENT

Regardless of the type of boss we're saddled with, we resent the relationship. Every time this person asks us to do something, even if it's done politely, we see red. We say, "Sure, Shirley, I'll get on it immediately," when we're really thinking, "Why don't you get off your lazy rump and do it yourself, you silly moron?!"

It's easy to see why bosses are perfect targets for hostility. No sooner do we exit our jobs than we release our pent-up anger for our bosses. We stop at our favorite watering hole for a couple of fast beers, and in the process of unwinding, we complain about our bosses to the bartender who is part-priest, part-rabbi, and all-around confidant. The perfect listener, he leans against the bar and cleans glasses, listening and nodding in respectful agreement. At appropriate times, he'll put in his pithy 2 cents: "It's a wonder you don't take a contract out on her. I don't know how you put up with her every day." From there, we go home and complain about our boss to our spouse, lover, kids, and anyone else who'll listen. And a variation of that cycle continues the next day and the day after that. Did I hit a responsive chord?

BOSS-WORKER RELATIONSHIPS ARE MORE COMPLICATED THAN YOU THINK

It's a sad fact of life, but most of us never get beyond a child-like relationship with our bosses, and all other authority figures for that matter. It has nothing to do with our ages, either. Whether 20 years old or 60 years old, we resent taking orders. Right or wrong, we blame our bosses because they're convenient and inescapable.

Seldom do we have a private talk with ourselves to explore the relationship and understand its dynamics so we can find out once and for all what irks us. *Advice:* The only way to make the relationship work is to examine it. As I said earlier, coexistence isn't enough. Getting through the day, like a schoolchild waiting for the three o'clock bell to ring, won't cut it. That's no way to live. Let's see if you can uncover the real issues and find an acceptable solution.

You might discover that your feelings are justified. You made the mistake of putting your boss on a pedestal. Like many others, you were taught to respect authority figures. Maybe your dad told you never to question your boss. Just shut up, take orders, and be happy you have a job. With that mindset, you assumed this person is right simply because he or she is the boss. What a relief to discover that this person is better suited to guard prisoners than to supervise white-collar professionals. And maybe you'll discover a few surprises as well.

QUICK SELF-TEST: FIRST-BASE ANALYSIS

WHOM DO YOU REALLY HATE? YOUR BOSS, YOUR JOB, OR BOTH?

The following painless questionnaire will tell you a lot about your feelings toward your job and boss. Be brutally honest. Nobody is going to see your answers.

1. Do you like the company?
2. If you answered *no*, what is it you dislike? The culture, people, work ethic?
3. Do you enjoy your job?
4. Did you settle by taking the job?
5. Why did you take it? Was it the job duties, money, both?
6. Do you like your boss?
7. If not, what is it you don't like about him or her? If yes, what do you admire about him or her?
8. How do you feel about taking orders?
9. Does your boss remind you of someone else? Whom?
10. If you could change something about your relationship with your boss, what would it be?

I tried this questionnaire out on a random sampling of people, and the answers were revealing. A 22-year-old male recent college graduate answered these questions about his first sales job this way:

1. No.
2. The whole shebang.
3. Not particularly.
4. I settled. I was being considered by three employers. This was the first offer that came along, so I grabbed it.
5. The main reason for taking the job was money. The bills were mounting, and I desperately needed a paycheck or I was in big trouble.
6. I can't stand him.
7. I don't like anything about him. He's opinionated, over-bearing, thoughtless, egotistical, and stupid. I don't even like the way he dresses.
8. I hate to take orders. Every time my boss tells me to do something, I cringe and pray he doesn't detect how I feel.

9. He reminds me of my high school physics teacher. He was a pompous academic who swore he had all the answers. He'd take points off your grade if you were late to class a certain number of times. He flunked me one semester. I've never forgotten or forgiven that guy.

10. My job. I've been looking for another job for 2 months. As soon as I find one that's an improvement, I'm outta here.

We can conclude this man is not having a positive work experience. But this man's problem is not his boss; it's his job. He hates his job so much that it's impossible for him to look with objectivity at anything connected to his employer. The boss is a symbol of the company and thus the perfect scapegoat. All he wants is out. He's not alone. Millions of others are in the same boat.

A 35-year-old female clothing buyer employed by a large department store gave these answers:

1. I'm not crazy about the company. It's a close-knit family operation that parcels out the best jobs to family members.

2. No matter how long you've been with the company, it's tough to get ahead.

3. I love my job.

4. I didn't settle at all.

5. I didn't know anything about family politics when I took the job. The money wasn't bad; it was the job description that hooked me.

6. I have no love for my boss.

7. Like me, he's not a family member. But the difference is that he's been with the company for 15 years. It's not his seniority that bothers me; it's that he's a backstabber who's always sucking up to family members. He doesn't care about anyone under him. All he cares about is looking good. To accomplish that end, he often takes credit for other people's work, including mine.

8. I have no problem taking orders as long as they make sense. In fact, I seek out direction and guidance. It helps me focus myself to be more productive. Some people are self-starters, but I need input from others.

9. My boss reminds me of some of the women I knew in college. Many were schemers totally out for themselves. Like my boss, they couldn't be trusted.

10. I really enjoy my job. I wish the power structure was different and I had a different boss. There is little question that, if my boss left, I'd have a better chance of moving up the ladder. But I don't see that happening. Eventually, I'll have to leave in order to get a better job. I'm just being practical.

Get the idea? As these answers show, it's important to examine how you feel about your job. Those sentiments could color your feelings about your boss. Like a doctor diagnosing an illness, you must know the origin of the symptoms.

Let's move on and find out what it takes to be a boss.

ANYONE CAN BE A BOSS— EVEN YOU!

He's so cold-blooded he would give the Mafia a bad name.

GENE PERRET

Funny Business, Prentice Hall

How many times have you heard someone say, "My boss doesn't know his———from his elbow?" Or more politely, "My boss doesn't have the foggiest idea what he's doing." In most cases, it's not just sour grapes from the mouths of disgruntled employees but rather the truth. The reason is simple: Many bosses are just plain incompetent. Yet, in bosses' defense, there are some logical reasons for such incompetence that are seldom considered by employees.

"YOU MEAN MY BOSS ISN'T GOD?"

The first assumption many of us make is thinking that bosses are deities. Today, it seems archaic, but you'd be surprised how many people grew up thinking that way. A second-generation American from East European peasant stock, I was one of them.

I remember my dad lecturing me about the secrets of holding down a job, which were passed on to him by his father. Those simple facts of working life included making an ally of your boss, doing what you're told, not getting on his or her wrong side, and whatever you do, not questioning the boss's judgment. Remember, he is the boss and that means he has special power which makes him right by his lofty position alone. Back then, they didn't know about empowerment, self-directed work teams, and the psychobabble taught in business schools about building harmonious working relationships between managers and employees. All of that express-your-inner-feelings, build-good-relationship stuff didn't exist. It was simply the boss is the boss and your job is to shut your mouth, not question authority, and do what you're told. Take it or leave it. If you have complaints, then find another job.

If you were trying to build a life during the Depression, as my father did, this career advice made perfect sense. The goal was not finding a challenging job that you loved, with built-in career potential and great benefits, but rather finding any job that paid a decent salary. In those troubled times, every job was the job. If you were lucky enough to find a decent job, you held onto it for dear life whether you liked it or not. As for your boss, it didn't matter if he acted like Attila the Hun and carried a bullwhip in his belt to motivate lazy employees. The goal was to do what you were told and get along with this person. As for loving your job, fellow workers, and the boss, these were inconsequential factors. If by some stroke of good fortune, you loved the whole shebang, you scored a touchdown.

In most cases, workers like my father learned to grin and bear it. They kept their mouths shut, did their jobs, and if they had a serious beef with their boss, either squelched their feelings or vented their frustration outside of the workplace. Transferring your hostility to your dog always worked. But airing your gripes to your boss face-to-face was definitely not a cool thing to do. In fact, it was a good way to get axed: "What do you mean I'm insensitive to your feelings and am not motivating you by giving you challenging, problem-solving tasks? Clear out your desk and turn in your keys. You're fired!"

In defense of those less than democratic, pre-World War II working conditions, millions of workers still managed to build harmonious working relationships and formidable careers. By a combination of sheer will and luck, they managed to hook up with decent bosses who took them under their wings and helped them realize their potential. But most people were not so lucky and had problems stemming from either their boss or the job itself.

WHO EVER SAID BOSSES KNOW WHAT THEY'RE DOING?

IT'S NOT ALL THEIR FAULT EITHER

The second dangerous assumption is thinking bosses actually know how to manage people. Mention the word *boss,* and we immediately think this person has some special abilities or training. When bosses make bad decisions, or even fools of themselves, we're horrified, amused, and pleased all at the same time. "Can you believe this guy is the boss, and he doesn't even know what he's doing? How did he ever get the job? Why, I could do better!"

Maybe you could. But there are logical reasons explaining how bosses get their jobs. How many people do you know who went to school to become a boss or dreamed of being a boss when they were kids? Many people grow up fantasizing about running their own business, but being a boss or manager? I don't think so. Consider the following facts about bosses.

The Job Carries No Qualifications.   There are rules and training programs for every job conceivable from sanitation engineer (garbage collector) to nuclear physicist, but there is no set curriculum that teaches you how to be a boss and no universal standards have been developed outlining how to perform this job.

Ninety-nine-pound weaklings don't become football linebackers, and ungainly klutzes rarely become tennis aces. It takes exceptional athletic ability to become a superstar athlete. Similarly, it takes special abilities, whether they be conceptual, creative, analytical, or computational skills, to be an engineer, mathematician, or architect. But there is no concrete set of skills necessary to be a boss. There are thousands of jobs that offer certification programs for advanced practitioners. But there are no such standards necessary for being a fair-minded, egalitarian boss.

While many large and mid-size companies provide training seminars and lectures for supervisors and middle managers, the majority of companies offer no training for bosses. And most of the so-called training programs are halfhearted attempts to teach specific managerial skills such as how to delegate authority, get feedback, and work with difficult employees. These programs are usually superficial. Can you teach someone to be a nurse, physical therapist, social worker, or psychologist in only 2 days? Imagine if there was an intensive 3-day program in cardiac surgery. Complete it with honors and you get a certificate that allows you to do state-approved open-heart surgery. Now there's a frightening thought.

On the corporate front, many accelerated training programs are just ploys by senior management to make the company seem progressive and in tune with the times. To do so, companies bring in high-priced management consultants who have written a couple of books to pass on their secrets on progressive management. The results are dismal.

A middle manager of a major pharmaceutical firm had this to say about his company's management seminars:

> They amounted to an expensive joke. We learned nothing concrete that would help us be better bosses. But as corporate outings, they were wildly successful. No expense was spared. At least once a year, the 3- or 4-day seminars were held in a special location. One year, it was an expensive resort in the North Carolina woods, another time it was a tiny island off the Florida coast, and last year, the company rented a luxurious ski lodge in Colorado. Wherever the location, they're always lavish affairs where 300 managers are flown in from all over the United States. Three hours a day, a prominent management consultant lectures us on improving productivity or techniques for bringing out the best in employees. Some managers don't even bother showing up, and those who do seldom take notes. Many are so hungover from drinking the night before that they hardly remember anything that's been said. The

majority of the managers who seem like they're attentively listening can't wait to get out in the sun to ski, golf, swim, or just have a good time. In short, our management seminars are no more than free drinking and eating orgies. We chalk the whole experience up to one of the fun perks of working for a Fortune 500 company.

Then there are the MBA-type professional managers who business schools love to brag about. They're praised as the new breed of managers. They're smart, schooled in the latest trendy management techniques, and supposedly tuned into the fast-paced workplace of the 1990s. While MBA training programs get great press, in actuality there aren't that many of them. When you look at the country as a whole, the MBA ranks are quite small. What does it matter how much the MBA graduate bosses know? Ninety-nine percent of the bosses will never enroll in an MBA program. What's more, most bosses don't even have a bachelor's degree. And slick business magazines like *Fortune* and *Forbes,* which are targeted at MBAs and other highly educated professionals, ignore many of the bread-and-butter issues facing the majority of bosses. The average boss couldn't tell you whether Peter Drucker or Tom Peters are management gurus or serial killers. Nor do they care.

Bosses Have Incompetent Role Models.   Bosses are not trained to be managers, and most had inadequate or poor role models. It can be likened to parenthood where we learn by example. Parents swear they're not going to make the same mistakes as their parents, yet most of them wind up doing the same things. We learn by example. It's the same story with bosses. How can anyone be a good boss if their role model was a high-strung megalomaniac who managed a department as if it were a military battalion?

John Trepan, manager of a 50-person department in a small Wyoming forestry firm, says he learned all the wrong techniques from his boss. Even worse, Trepan didn't realize he wasn't a good boss until morale suffered and he lost three of his best workers to competitors. He says:

When my boss moved up the ladder and promoted me to his former job, I did whatever he did and assumed it was the only way to run a department. I found out otherwise. He was an authoritarian who was distant, demanding, aloof, and he rarely communicated with any of the people under him. He gave an order and expected it to be executed with no questions asked. If a task wasn't completed properly, rather than sit down with a worker and show him how to do it correctly, he humiliated him in front of other workers.

I am ashamed to say that I did the same thing. When I took over the department, my coworkers expected me to be an improvement from our former boss. I disappointed them by pulling a Dr. Jekyll and Mr. Hyde number. One day, I was one of them; the next day, I was their boss, a mean-spirited son of a bitch. Six months later, I realized that a good boss doesn't rule with an iron fist, but rather with understanding, compassion, communication, and shared goals. When morale and productivity fell and my big producers suddenly quit with only a week's notice, I knew I had a problem. A couple of weeks after one of my best workers left, I accidentally ran into him at a local shopping mall. Upset about his leaving, I asked him why he took another job. Secure in a new position, he unloaded the truth on me. It felt like he had opened fire with a shotgun at point-blank range. Pulling no punches, he told me I was abusive, inconsiderate, inconsistent, and had lost all sense of compassion for people I had known for years. In the space of a few months, I managed to alienate everyone who worked for me. At first I was sorry I spoke to my former employee, but afterwards I was glad I did it. I thanked him, apologized, and we went our separate ways. Until he told me the uncensored truth, I had no idea I was a horror-story boss.

After Trepan had that heart-to-heart discussion, he started mending his ways. It was reminiscent of Charles Dickens's *A Christmas Carol,* in which the sickly Tiny Tim taught Ebenezer Scrooge that he was a mean and miserly man who didn't care about anyone but himself. To his workers' surprise, Trepan changed his behavior the very next day. What's more, he started reading management books and enrolled in management courses at a nearby business college.

Unfortunately, not all bosses experience this fairy-talelike catharsis. Most bad boss scenarios end with employees either being canned, quitting, or on a few rare occasions, beating their bosses to a pulp. A handful of evil bosses have been murdered by disgruntled employees, a course of action this writer discourages. No matter how much you hate your boss, winding up on death row is not a good solution.

Bosses Misuse or Abuse Authority. From the true story I just cited, it's easy to see how bosses can abuse authority. One day, you're just another worker taking orders and griping about the power chain; the next, you're a boss with people reporting to you. Not only must employees now take orders from you, you're also the one they must please. It doesn't matter whether you're in charge of 1 or 100 people; as soon as a person has to report to and answer to someone else, you have a boss-employee relationship. Any first-time boss will tell you that the first surge of power is a pretty heady feeling. Former Secretary of State Henry Kissinger described power as "the great aphrodisiac." In *The Light and the Dark* (1961), writer C.P. Snow had this to say about power: "No man is fit to be trusted with power... Any man who has lived at all knows the follies and wickedness he's capable of."

One of the best descriptions of the boss-worker relationship can be found in *Power,* Michael Korda's indictment of power-hungry corporate cultures. Says Korda, "The average corporation functions as a kind of broker, providing those who want power with a certain number of people over whom they can exert it. This costs nothing; every organization always has plenty of people so unimportant or easily replaceable...that it is simply enough to satisfy the power cravings of even the most incompetent executive by giving them someone to tyrannize. For years, this has been the real function of secretaries in the minds of many men."

Over the past two centuries, there have been countless cases of bosses terrorizing their secretaries. When not bullying them, they're demanding sexual favors in return for job security. Even today, with widespread awareness of diversity issues, Equal Employment Opportunity Commission legislation, and a plethora of publicity about sexual harassment, women often still pay a mighty price for prosecuting their bosses. Although they receive well-earned satisfaction in fighting back, the majority of whistle-blowers wind up losing their jobs in the bargain.

It's easy to let power go to your head. Many bosses use it as a weapon to compensate for their inadequacies, frustrations, and failures; others use it to cast a spell of fear and anxiety in the ranks. It happens in all companies, but especially in small ones. This is where you find the prototypical big fish in little ponds who couldn't cut it in larger organizations with complex and strict reporting relationships. In small companies, however, these petty bureaucrats, many of whom have been victimized by tyrannical bosses, can be king of the mountain, wreaking fear, panic, and emotional suffering on everyone in their charge. They get off knowing they're dreaded, and their employees' jobs depend on pleasing them.

Bosses Often Operate with Complete Autonomy. If you have worked for any length of time in a company, it's easy to understand how bosses get away with tyrannical behavior. If you think there are checks and balances on most of them, you're dead wrong. The majority of bosses in small companies have almost complete autonomy. They're like feudal lords, free to run their fiefdoms as they please. They can be enlightened despots, vicious dictators, or democratic leaders considerate of their troops. It's the luck of the draw.

Small companies, in particular, are guilty of producing more bad bosses than their mid-size and large company counterparts. That's because the average small company, which has fewer than 500 workers, is a tightly run, yet often under-staffed, operation. The chain of command is not concerned with monitoring its managers but simply with boosting productivity.

Tom Perry, an admittedly tough supervisor in a Philadelphia apparel company, described how the reporting relationship and power structure worked at his 130-person company.

> I've been with the company 18 years. I started out as a stock clerk and worked my way up through the ranks. I found my stride when

I was promoted to a sales job. When the president saw that I had selling ability and could capture accounts, the waters parted and I was given increased responsibility. When I was named the biggest producer in my region, I was promoted to regional sales manager in charge of 20 salespeople and three administrative staff members. Until then, I had never been in charge of one person, no less 23. I saw this as my opportunity to make a name for myself and boost my career. By pounding on doors selling, I knew that the key to keeping my job and hopefully moving up was getting the "numbers" [conquering new accounts]. I never actually thought about the people reporting to me. All I knew was that they were a reflection on me. I saw them as an extension of myself. If they did well, I looked good. I never thought about whether they were happy or treated well. When my salespeople returned from the field with new accounts, I was delighted. If they returned empty-handed, I was furious. I didn't want to hear excuses. All I cared about were results, and I didn't care how they got them.

Perry's boss wasn't much different. Tom continues:

My boss never told me how to manage people, nor did he ever look over my shoulder and give me pointers. He reasoned that if he figured out how to run a company, I could certainly learn how to manage a small department. The only time I heard from my boss was when he commented on my department's performance. When the numbers were up significantly, I was praised, and when the numbers were off slightly, I was told to boost them. He never asked about the people reporting to me. It was almost like they weren't human. It sounds horrible, but that's pretty much how I related to them. My employees were tiny cogs in the company machinery. If they stopped performing well, I replaced them without any second thoughts. Everyone was expendable, including myself. Like the other managers at the company, I was looking out for number one: myself.

Perry is a coldhearted guy, yet he's no different from thousands of other managers. They're all playing their own variations on the survival game. To protect their jobs, there are going to be casualties. Naturally, they don't intend to be one of them.

Bosses Operate in a Vacuum Without Feedback from Employees.   I've spoken to dozens of people who report having excellent relationships with their bosses. Most of them work for progressive mid-size companies that pride themselves on cultivating open communication lines between managers and employees. Curiously, many are second- and third-generation family-owned companies that were founded by the boss's father or grandfather, many of whom had barely completed high school, no less college. Many were traditional authoritarian managers. Most were tough and demanding, but fair. Their progeny, however, went to business school to learn modern management techniques so they could take over the firms and successfully pilot them into the twenty-first century. Many sound like they walked out of the exclusive Wharton School at the University of Pennsylvania. A fair share have MBA degrees. Ask them about their management techniques, and they will sprinkle their conversation with 1990s buzz terms such as "empowered workers" and "self-directed work teams." They have their own spin on TQM (total quality management) and how to achieve it, and they've all read books by the leading gurus of modern management. Five days a week, they religiously skim, if not read, *The Wall Street Journal*.

While "New Age" managers are in the minority, most of them have chalked up impressive results. By applying the theories of Michael Hammer, Robert Waterman, and Tom Peters and by forging a partnership between workers and managers, they not only boost productivity but create democratic working environments where employees actually enjoy their jobs.

Yet most bosses don't know about or care about progressive management techniques. They insist it smacks of phoniness and are content to remain in the Dark Ages. One old-line manager in a 50-person New Jersey metal fabricating plant put it this way: "What's the point of using all those stupid management techniques? I don't want to know what my workers think. I've got a good relationship with my people. I'm not about to ask them their opinions about anything. I call the shots, and that's the way it's always been. It's just plain old respect. The workers like it that way. The proof of the pudding is we do good work and we've been doing it for 25 years. Like they say, if it ain't broke, why fix it?"

But even bosses such as this manager would change if they were able to see themselves through their employees' eyes. Similar to the Scroogelike John Trepan cited earlier, their behavior might embarrass them into mending their ways.

WHAT HAPPENS TO BAD BOSSES? BAD BOSS CLINIC OR A SLAP ON THE WRIST?

ANSWER: NOT MUCH

Just as there are no set training programs for bosses, there is no universal solution for dealing with problem bosses who are brought to the attention of company owners or chief executives. Unlike delinquent drivers compelled to attend driver clinics to learn safe driving techniques, there is no sanitarium for bad bosses.

Bosses that perform well can practically coast through their entire career wreaking havoc among employees. The only time bad bosses are called on the carpet is when they embarrass their boss by doing something stupid (such as making fools of themselves at a company event), when named in a sexual harassment suit, or when embroiled in corporate politics.

Typically, the first two cases are handled with a mild slap on the wrist. Getting blotto at a Christmas party might draw a disapproving, "Jean, your people are going to stop respecting you if you pull a stunt like that again" or "There were a couple of important clients at that party. Please curb your drinking next time and think about the poor image it creates for the company." A sexual harassment suit is more serious. "Pete, we've got a problem here. I've turned the matter over to our attorney who's confident this situation can be handled out of court. It's going to cost us money to keep this thing quiet. We can't have this happen again."

A high-performing boss who is caught up in corporate politics may be handled differently. Small-company heads often use discussion, arbitration, or mediation so warring factions can find a common ground leading to a harmonious working relationship. The trend among mid-size and large companies is to hire executive coaches to shadow the boss and work one-on-one, fine-tuning the boss's interpersonal skills. Many companies pay between $35,000 and $80,000 to upgrade their bosses' people skills. It sounds like a lot of money to squander on teaching skills the bosses should have possessed before they were hired. As one high-ranking executive at a thriving mid-size company explained it: "It's bottom-line reasoning all the way. If a top manager is bringing in a million dollars of business a year, it's worth it to quell disharmony in the ranks by hiring an executive coach. If there is a fire burning, a crisis of confidence, or a tremendous rift in the management team, the brass will do everything possible to hold on to a top producer. You can't blame them."

In an effort to build superstar bosses with CEO potential, some large companies send their fast-trackers away to leadership or management camps for several days. There they learn how to take "feedback" and "synergize." The nonprofit Center for Creative Leadership in Colorado Springs, for example, charges $7400 for a 5-day course. Executives get "360-degree feedback" in which a manager's strengths and weaknesses are evaluated through lengthy questionnaires filled out by bosses, subordinates, and peers.

If you're wondering how they stomach 12 hours of psychobabble a day, a well-stocked bar and a six-figure salary make it easier.

FOUR REASONS
PEOPLE BECOME BOSSES

Once you understand how people become bosses, you'll understand why demon bosses aren't fired so quickly. I hate to smash icons, but most people don't become bosses because they have proven managerial skills. Rather, they get ahead for one of the following four reasons.

1. *Politics.*   Some of us are better than others at playing organizational games. Many bosses, especially high-ranking ones in large companies, are masters at it. Read the biographies of superstar CEOs—the likes of Lee Iacocca, Andrew Carnegie, and Henry Ford—and you'll discover that they were visionary politicians. They played people as they would pawns on a chessboard, strategically and thoughtfully planned. They had a knack for analyzing organizational maps and piloting themselves to the executive suite. They befriended the power players and cautiously stepped over dissenters and trouble-makers on their way up. On that long, steep road to the top, they captured more and more power.

2. *Nepotism.*   A close cousin to politics is nepotism, the practice of paying back a favor or a good turn with a job or a promotion. Nepotism has been practiced since the beginning of time. Your best buddy turned you on to the company that hired you. Three years later, you've been promoted to vice president, and you need someone to take over your old job of running a 40-person office staff. So you call your friend, who just happens to be out of a job, and ask him if he's interested. Naturally, he jumps at the opportunity. Favor repaid. What does it matter if the friend never managed an office staff in his entire career? This wasn't an issue for the newly appointed vice president. His feeling was, "He'll learn on the job, the way I did."

Nepotism is a powerful force in any organization. The frightening part is that extraordinary jobs carrying enormous responsibilities are given away because of it.

3. *Special abilities, skills, education.*   Special skills have never been more important. Technical skills, especially, are critical to all companies. Consider the experience of software wizard Howard Slone.

Slone was hired by a Los Angeles computer game company

because he was a talented programmer. At the time, the company knew nothing about his creative abilities. Eight months after starting, Slone knocked on his boss's door, begging for 15 minutes of time. He told him that he just developed what he thought was a neat *Star Wars*-like game for computer buffs. It could be easily loaded into any computer and was the kind of game that's addictive because it tests the player's reflexes. Slone's boss wasn't thrilled about interrupting a report he was working on, but he felt obliged to comply because he had heard good things about Slone. Slone loaded the game into his boss's computer and then asked his boss to follow the simple commands. At first, his boss grimaced politely. But hardly 30 seconds later, he was immersed in the game. He was addicted. He pushed aside the report he was working on and practically forgot that Slone was looking over his shoulder watching him play the game. Twenty minutes passed before his boss spun around in his chair, smiled broadly at Slone, and said, "This is brilliant, Howard. It's hypnotic; it's extraordinary. It'll make a bloody fortune."

The topper was that Slone told him he developed the game on his own time. On several occasions, he worked straight through the night programming it. Suddenly, Slone became a prized commodity. On the very next day, he was pulled off his project and asked to head a team that would prepare the game for mass production and design the promotional package that would sell it. Six months later, Slone's game was sold in computer software stores throughout the United States. When the game racked up revenues of $10 million, Slone was made chief software designer in charge of 10 programmers. His technical skills catapulted him to a managerial slot.

Slone was a brilliant software designer, yet he fell far short of the mark as a boss. One of his early hires, a fresh-out-of-college programmer, had this to say about him:

> If someone had warned me about Howard, I would never have taken the job. Looking back, it seemed like I walked right into hell. I should have known the moment I met Howard that problems lie ahead. The man had no social graces. Calling him a bore

was a compliment. Why, he barely shook my hand before asking me a battery of questions. What I thought would be a friendly information exchange turned into a stress interview. Before he could even get a reading on my personality, he was trying to figure out what I could do. He didn't see me as a human being, but as a piece of equipment or an extension of a computer. I was human software. I could understand his wanting to find the right skills, but I found it odd that he didn't want to get a sense of me as a person.

It was during my first week on the job when I realized Howard was ruthlessly obsessed about getting results. Biweekly staff meetings were like being back in school with a tough professor who drilled us and made us squirm if we didn't return the right answers. The programmers sat around a long conference table while Howard stood at one end and fired questions to see how much we knew about a certain problem. If he had circulated a memo telling us something about the problem, we could have prepared ourselves. But that wasn't Howard's style. Instead, he delighted in putting us on the spot. He loved to watch us sweat and turn beet red with embarrassment when we didn't know the answers. If someone returned what he thought was a ridiculous answer, he'd embarrass them by saying something like, "Are you sure you have a degree in computer science? Did you sleep with the dean?"

When he was finished making jokes at our expense, he gave us the specifications on a project, assigned tasks, and set deadlines. The way it worked was each of us had a piece of the project. It was kind of like a jigsaw puzzle. Each piece had to fit into the next, so timing was critical. The point is that Howard never gave us enough information. He could have made our lives easier by providing guidelines, tips, and shortcuts. Instead, he delighted in making us uncomfortable and creating enormous anxiety. The irony was that we were supposed to be working as a team brainstorming for a common goal. Instead, we each went our separate ways to solve our own piece of the puzzle. Howard was a sadist who delighted in stumping us. He was exceptionally talented and expected everyone to perform at his level, which was ludicrous. Inevitably, we had to ask for extensions on projects because they were always too difficult.

The game we played was seeing how much we coud take before we quit. One programmer boasted that he endured Howard for 3 years. He figured that was worth an entry in *The Guiness Book of World Records*. After 1 year, I left for another job. I remember turning crimson on my job interview when asked about my prior boss. I skirted the issue by talking about the type of assignments I was given and the pressure of meeting tight deadlines. Before I could get into details, the interviewer knew I was avoiding talking about Howard, who had already ascended to legendary status in the industry. He was known as one of the worst bosses in the software industry.

How does Howard Slone keep his job? Simple. The president adores him because he always gets results—even if he almost drives his employees to the brink of suicide.

4. *Hard work/great attitude.* Finally, the combination of hard work and a great attitude is another powerful reason why some people become bosses. All employers want loyal hardworking employees on whom they can count. These are serious career-minded people who don't gripe about putting in extra hours. In fact, they willingly volunteer to do so. If there is a tight deadline, if a couple of staff members are out sick, or if a rush presentation has to be developed, they'll work through the night or give up a weekend to get the job done. They're willing to pitch in, no questions asked. Their job takes precedence over their personal lives. Their dedication, loyalty, and Puritan work ethic often get them promoted to supervisory jobs. Yet, they are no more qualified to be bosses than Howard Slone was. If they're reasonably healthy people willing to learn, they stand a chance of being decent bosses. Yet, if their gray matter is awry, watch out. It's a crapshoot.

Put it all together and you're left with an obvious conclusion: Anyone, including yourself, can be a boss. Pretty scary. Now meet some bosses from hell.

BOSSES FROM HELL

CAN YOU PICK YOUR BOSS OUT OF THE LINEUP?

Knowing that anyone can be a boss doesn't soften the reality that millions of hellish bosses are out there making people's lives miserable. Some of them ought to be locked up. A few are irredeemable, so why not toss the key?

You're going to meet some of them in this chapter. I guarantee they will sound chillingly familiar. See if you can pick your boss out of the lineup.

Ready? Brace yourself. I want you to read this section cold turkey without booze, tranquilizers, or illegal substances. In what follows, you may have a reunion with some bosses from your past, triggering memories you'd rather repress. Even more horrific, you may meet your present boss.

Recognizing the nemeses of your life is the first step. Later on, we'll learn how to deal with them. The bosses that follow range from garden variety neurotics to deviant wackos of psychotic proportions.

SICKO BOSSES

1. DEVIANT BOSSES

Let's lead off with the worst of the bunch. Deviant bosses delight in wreaking havoc. If you were to let your fantasies run wild, these are the folks you'd gladly sentence to a lifetime behind bars with no chance of parole. The four most common deviant bosses are:

Mind-Controlling Abusers.   In the post–Industrial Revolution days, physically abusive bosses were commonplace in factories across the United States. They'd work their charges until they were about ready to keel over from exhaustion. Workers were forced to meet backbreaking production quotas. If they failed to pull their weight, they were punched, poked, and prodded until they picked up the pace. The histories of the coal, steel, and automobile industries are full of these physically abusive bosses.

More common, regardless of the work settings or time period, are sexually abusive bosses. Many bosses are very clever at cajoling sexual favors from vulnerable employees. It's especially easy if you lack basic moral and ethical standards. Unsophisticated workers burdened with family responsibilities are ripe fodder for deviant bosses demanding sexual favors in return for job security. If workers refuse, they either lose their job or are given enough work to keep two people busy from dawn to dusk. And if they dare to complain to management, their life will be turned into a living hell.

Some abusive bosses enjoy controlling their employees by playing mental games with them. It can be likened to psychological torture. First, they feign interest so they can determine employees' strong and weak points. Then they play with them as if they were dolls. One day, they buoy their spirits by praising their work; the next day, they go for their jugular by attacking their weak points. These abusive bosses are masterful control freaks because they've learned how to turn their workers on and off like faucets. They are feared for good reason. Never knowing what kind of mood their bosses will be in when they arrive in the morning, captive employees live in constant fear. A 15-year veteran technician of a Florida jewelry company described what it was like working for such a boss:

We never knew what to expect. If our boss was in a good mood, it was like a blessing. The sun shined on the 200-person company. But if he was in a bad mood, it was as if a cloud hung over the place signaling an impending storm. Each worker hoped he'd stay clear of him or her. When he went after someone, he was merciless. He was all over this person. He knew how to get to every one of us. He even knew personal details that he'd use to humiliate us in front of other workers. One morning, he attacked the work of a 24-year-old woman who had been having an affair with one of the guys on the loading dock. He called her a whore who has no self-respect and said if she spent her nights resting rather than sleeping with all the men in town, her work would be a lot better.

There's one key reason why the woman took it and didn't tell the abusive boss where to go: She needed the job, as did many people at the company. Says the technician, "None of us had a heck of a lot of options. There aren't that many jobs to be had in this tiny coastal town. None of us could risk getting fired and going on unemployment. That's certainly not enough to live on if you've got a family to support."

Alcoholics and Drug Abusers.   Many bosses, burdened with stress and anxiety from numbing deadlines and production quotas, become dependent on alcohol and drugs. Incredibly, some rule with an iron fist for years before they either burn out or explode in a shattering nervous or physical breakdown. A small minority get drug or alcohol counseling either on their own or through their companies. But until they do, they make the lives of everyone around them miserable. To cope with pressure, they ply themselves with massive amounts of alcohol or drugs. One supervisor I spoke with in a small Ohio toy company said that during their peak production season, which is 6 months prior to Christmas, he would often consume a liter of vodka every day to get through the grueling 12-hour shifts. Says this boss, "Alcohol was the only thing that got me through those long days. My stress level was so high that it calmed me down. I'd usually start drinking after lunch and keep at it until I left at 9 or 10 p.m. Everyone knew I drank, but they had the good sense to keep their mouths shut or else I'd make their lives miserable." But when his personal life began to deteriorate, this supervisor was smart enough to see a therapist and join Alcoholics Anonymous.

A one-time hotshot Chicago stock trader in charge of a 20-person speculative trading unit discovered cocaine was the short-term secret to maintaining his fast-track lifestyle. By the time this 28-year-old trader was promoted to manager, he was the brokerage house's biggest producer. A securities analyst who worked under the broker remembered the young man's ascent to the fast lane:

Making him a supervisor was the stupidest thing the firm could have done. This was the last person who should have been in charge of people. It was all he could do to keep his own career together and manage himself, no less monitor other workers. Few people could maintain his pace and survive. He got up at 5 a.m. every day so he could take the 6:15 a.m. train to downtown Chicago. By the time he stormed into the office at 7:30 or 8 a.m., he had already digested *The Wall Street Journal,* the *Chicago Times,* and was well into *Investor's Daily.* No sooner did the opening bell sound than he was in perpetual motion until closing.

For most of the day, he was hell to work with. Things were bad enough before he started using cocaine. Back then, he was just revved up on coffee, which he consumed all day. By 2 p.m., he had usually consumed about eight cups of coffee and he was good for a half dozen more before he left. But when the coffee was fueled with cocaine, things got dangerously out of hand. Coffee kept him wired and active, but cocaine turned him into a whirling dervish intent on destroying anything in his path. All day long, he'd storm through the office shouting orders. He'd walk up to my desk and demand an analysis of a certain stock. If I didn't deliver it to him in 10 minutes, he would have a temper tantrum. He pulled the same tactics with others. There was no delivering information fast enough.

As his intake of cocaine increased, he got worse. When he first started using the drug, he'd discreetly exit to the men's room where he snorted the coke from a little decongestant bottle he carried with him. But when he realized he was losing precious time with his bathroom trips, he simply pulled the antihistamine bottle from his pocket in the office and snorted coke all day long. He figured everyone would think he had a bad cold. We all knew that it was no over-the-counter remedy he was sucking up his nose. After 6 months of nonstop cocaine use, his nose dripped constantly because the nasal membranes were burned out.

The man was pathetic. If he wasn't so horrible and obnoxious, we might have felt sorry for him. But he was impossible. Just before he collapsed and entered a drug rehabilitation program, he was out of control and couldn't remember what he did from one moment to the next. He'd scream an order and then 15 seconds later repeat it, forgetting that it had been executed immediately. Then all hell would break loose.

Sadists.   The cruelest of the deviant bosses are the sadists. These bosses delight in inflicting psychological pain. They've taken power to a dangerous level. If this were the fourteenth century, they'd be taking troublesome employees to the dungeon and torturing them. Maybe that's a slight exaggeration, but suffice it to say that sadistic bosses get off by making people miserable. You don't have to be a psychotherapist to figure out how they got that way. Most are getting back for the abuse heaped on them. Some were the product of authoritarian homes where stern parents delighted in verbally or physically abusing them when they were kids. Other sadistic bosses had to endure their own abusive bosses and are now taking what they consider to be well-earned revenge. And still others are using their power to express their contempt for humanity. Some sadistic bosses are misanthropes of Olympian proportions.

Sadistic bosses come in two varieties. One enjoys private displays of sadism; the other prefers exhibitionist displays. The former will either corner a worker alone or ask to see her in his office. Then he levels the bad news by expressing disgust and contempt for her work. To rectify bad performance, he may insist that 2 weeks of grueling work be redone or that redemption be earned by putting in 2 to 3 hours of overtime every night.

The latter boss usually practices sadism in meetings, which often prove to be a ready forum for power-crazed bosses to reduce their employees to shaking, quivering, blubbering masses before their colleagues. A high-ranking senior editor in a Boston national magazine describes how her editor in chief used meetings as a platform for her sadism:

Not a single editor wasn't terrified of the weekly staff meetings. As soon as she was promoted to editor in chief, we all knew our lives would be miserable. One of the first things she did was change the meeting day from Wednesday to Monday morning at 9:30 a.m., which tells you a lot about her personality. The former editor in chief had felt Wednesday was a good meeting day because it gave editors time to come down from the weekend and gather their story ideas. Our new boss had other ideas. She figured there was no better way to ruin our weekends than by creating instant anxiety the moment we walked in on Monday morning. Most of us had to start getting ready for the Monday morning torture on Sunday evening, which was pretty depressing. On Monday, we all came to work nervous and uptight about what was ahead. We had good reason to be afraid because every meeting inevitably turned into a head-bashing ritual. It was just a question of how many people she'd attack.

The meetings were pretty straightforward. Each editor came in with story ideas that either they originated or were suggested by freelance writers with whom we worked. Sitting around an oval table, the editor in chief asked us each to stand and discuss the two or three ideas we thought were worthy of an article assignment. Having given a 3-minute spiel on each idea, we then waited for everyone's comments and, finally, the last word from our boss who we appropriately dubbed Eva Braun. Sometimes the comments from our fellow editors were a little cruel or hostile, but they paled in comparison to the remarks of our boss.

She hated bulletproof queries, ideas that were solid original stories worthy of assignment, because then she had nothing to rail against and was forced to nod her ahead in agreement. Nevertheless, she managed to find plenty of material to attack. When she did, she was like a starved cheetah hungrily ripping her prey apart. She relished every minute of it. We wondered why she didn't drool and salivate while she took bite-sized pieces out of an editor. As soon as she heard fragments of what she thought was a dumb idea, she went to town on the editor with a vengeance. In less than a minute, she criticized, insulted, ridiculed, and systematically tore apart the editor's credibility. A common attack went like this: "You've got to be joking with that idea, Jack. You must have thought that one up as you rode in on the subway. It's dumb. Do you really want to insult our readers with a story like that? They get that kind of fluff in the tabloids. They're not going to get it from us. You have got to tell us, Jack, seriously, what were you thinking when you came up with that idea? I don't pay you a great salary for crap like that. You're a senior editor; start thinking like one. If you can't do better than that, I'll get some smart-assed kid just out of grad school and I guarantee he'll come up with better ideas."

If that's not bad enough, she'd become more abusive if you disagreed with her in front of the other editors. Then it was no holds barred, and she'd go on to attack your family, friends, religion, politics, or just about anything else that popped into her head. On occasions, the editor in chief's verbal attacks were so heated that some editors ran out of the room crying, while others started stammering because they were so nervous.

Predator Bosses.   This term was coined by management consultant Harvey Hornstein in his book *Brutal Bosses and Their Prey*. Hornstein identified three species of predator bosses: "The Conqueror," "The Performer," and "The Manipulator."

Conqueror bosses prey on employees who show signs of weakness, according to Hornstein. Their destructive skill is their ability to treat the workplace like a battlefield. Once predator bosses uncover someone's Achilles heel, they go after it with a vengeance. The unsuspecting victim is now putty in that person's hands. Conqueror bosses particularly relish honing in on weaknesses that are a source of embarrassment and humiliation.

A junior architect who stutters when under intense pressure was ripe prey for her conqueror boss. As soon as her boss heard the architect stammer a few times at a weekly meeting, she became a target for his depravity. Cruelly, he went after her at public meetings, never one-on-one. On one occasion, the boss attacked her presentation by saying the architect did a shoddy job by not adequately preparing her work beforehand. When the architect tried to defend herself, she began to stammer uncontrollably. Every time she tried to get out a word, the boss would say something like, "Your friends and shrink forgive your neurotic affliction, but I don't have all day to wait for you to spit a thought out. I'm trying to run a profit center; I don't have time to play occupational therapist. So de-de-de ya-ya th-th-th-think ya-ya can just express one thought before we break for lunch?" Sometimes the boss would embarrass the poor worker for 15 to 20 minutes until someone got him on to a different subject.

Hornstein says victims can survive their conqueror bosses by studying the patterns of their predators. "Don't stop in the area where they're hunting," warns Hornstein. Easier said than done. Sometimes it is unavoidable, such as in the case just cited. That conqueror cleverly set up his victim by trapping her in meetings. The only way out was excusing herself, thus admitting defeat. That would not only make her a bigger target for her boss but would also make her look bad in front of her coworkers. Her only salvation was to overprepare for meetings, maintain her cool, and pray her boss didn't go after her. Still, she lived in fear of him, never knowing when she'd be attacked.

Performer bosses also have a penchant for belittling workers, says Hornstein. Unlike conqueror bosses, who enjoy dominating their workers, performer bosses undermine workers to mask their own incompetence. Hornstein warns that trying to reason with them can backfire. They've been known to have uncontrollable temper tantrums and even throw things at workers. The best defense, advises Hornstein, is to stay clear of them.

Manipulators are the smoothest of the predator bosses. Hornstein cites the boss that Sigourney Weaver plays in the film *Working Girl* as a dramatic example. Weaver portrayed a refined, sophisticated, and very polished boss who had her sights set on the executive suite. She seemed polite and considerate and gave the impression that she cared about her workers. Yet it was only a well-rehearsed act. She met her match in a secretary (played by Melanie Griffith) who was smarter than she was. Hornstein says manipulator bosses are afraid they'll become less valued if their underlings get the limelight, or any recognition for that matter. They'll go to any end to retain their power. They'll lie or even reject a subordinate's idea and then take credit for it and never give you credit. They'll always appear to be the subordinate's ally. In reality, however, they wouldn't think twice about backstabbing their staff members and walking over the corpses for a coveted trophy.

Hornstein isn't kidding when he says manipulator bosses can be deadly. *Advice:* Watch your back.

2. PSYCHOTIC BOSSES

There is no shortage of psychotic bosses either. Contrasted to the neurotic ones, many of the psychotic variety are a short step away from being institutionalized. It would be to everyone's advantage, especially the employees who report to them, if they were taken off the street and put in a hospital. Now there's a utopian concept. Here are a few common varieties.

Schizophrenic Bosses. *The Oxford English Dictionary* defines schizophrenia as "a form of mental illness in which the personality is disintegrated and detached from its environment." An abbreviated definition is "split-mind." Put these folks in a supervisory position and their poor employees never know what they're going to get. They're forced to deal with Jekyll and Hyde behavior, which amounts to a terrifying proposition.

Going to work every day can be likened to entering the gates of heaven or the depths of hell, depending on whether the boss is eliciting Jekyll or Hyde behavior. Everything is great when the boss is in the Dr. Jekyll phase. He or she is alert, considerate, and thoughtful. But if the tables are turned and employees are greeted by Mr. Hyde, watch out! They can look forward to brutal ridicule and abuse.

Making matters worse, schizoid bosses frequently undergo radical personality shifts during the business day. Their personalities change as unexpectedly as the wind. An event (poor sales returns, aggressive competitors), an insubordinate employee, or a reaming from his or her boss can turn the tides. It feels as if a twister of killer proportions begins to destroy everything in its path. Suddenly, workers are hurled into a state of panic and fear.

An administrative assistant employed by a Los Angeles accounting firm worked for a boss just like this. She describes his radical personality shift:

> After working for the man for 8 years, I could sense it coming. It was as if something was in the air. Sometimes all it took was a phone call. Often, a senior executive triggered the change. You could hear my boss's voice change on the phone. A sort of built-in self-protection mechanism kept him in check with his boss. As crazy as he was, he knew that if the boss saw his lunatic side, he'd be on the unemployment line. Like a kid holding his breath, he waited to unleash his madness on the people below him. He knew we'd keep our mouths shut because we feared for our jobs. But it was the look in his eyes and the way he stalked the halls that told us the mad side of his personality had taken over. His eyes were tense, unblinking, and scanning the office for targets. His gait was brisk, agitated, and swift. His poor victims never knew what was happening.

She says that if she was lucky, she'd be called into his office and reamed. More commonly, he'd launch a full-scale attack in front of 100 other workers.

> The thought of finding a discreet place and time never occurred to him. Only a rational, fairly healthy person would consider those things. Most always, he attacked employees for incompetence and ingeniously spun some incredible story about how they were ripping off the company. He'd wind up saying something like, "You'd better get your act together or else I'll find someone who really wants the job." And then he'd toss in a little well-placed guilt with, "You know how many people would kill to have your job? Think about that before you pull this kind of shenanigan again." The solution to my

boss's tantrums was obvious. Knowing the cues and sensing the erupting tornado, we hit the decks and made ourselves scarce. An hour or two later, his psychotic outbreak dissipated as quickly as it had erupted. Then it was back to normal. His face would lighten, his body would relax, and he was Mr. Nice Guy again.

Bosses like this ought to be locked up in padded cells. The problem is there aren't enough mental institutions around the country to hold all of them.

Manic-Depressive Bosses.   Equally confounding and frightening are manic-depressive bosses. They display split personalities of a different, but no less disturbing, kind. Rather than displaying short bouts of madness, manic-depressives can go days, even weeks, in one state. Just as their name implies, manic phases are bombastic high-energy states. Manic bosses are omnipresent. Their presence is felt even when they're not in the room. Full of energy, they're cheering their troops on. At social gatherings, however, they often make spectacles of themselves. They often drink too much and draw attention to themselves by speaking too loudly and telling unfunny, crude jokes. A machinist at a Vermont lumber company describes his manic-depressive boss at an annual Christmas party:

> This guy was like a wind-up toy. He came wired, but all it took were two gin and tonics to downshift this guy into overdrive. He danced with every woman regardless of whether or not they wanted to. Then he embarrassed himself by attempting Fred Astaire-like routines. He was pathetic. I felt sorry for the women because all they wanted to do was escape. But the topper was when he started coming on to his boss's wife. He danced with her and held her inappropriately. When she tried to get clear of him, he kept on being persistent. If it weren't for a couple of managers who pulled him out of the place and took him home, I'm convinced the president would have decked him and then fired him.

What's striking about manic-depressives is their behavior extremes. People who have endured manic-depressive bosses say there is never any question about which state their boss is in. Whereas the manic state is a high-energy out-of-control phase, the depressive state is marked by almost complete with-drawal. Bosses in a depressive state crawl into their own shell, purposely avoiding employees, even their own bosses. Some disappear for days at a time. Others withdraw to the safety of their homes, afraid of running into anyone who knows them. Their productivity slips, and they rely on their workers to carry the workload.

A salesman working for a Detroit greeting card company describes his manic-depressive boss:

> If we had a choice, we preferred our boss's manic state. He was loud and wired, but at least he was productive. When he was severely depressed, no one saw him. Most of us felt sorry for him, so we covered for him by making excuses. We made decisions for him. In fact, his secretary often forged his signature on memos and letters, saving his job on occasions. When he wasn't function-ing, he was a burden and we all had to do more than our share.

The solution for psychotic bosses boils down to three words: They need help. A conservative guess is that less than 5 percent of psychotic bosses actually get help, whether it be psychotherapy, group therapy, or a support group. Many schizophrenic and manic-depressive bosses should be med-icated so they can function with some degree of normalcy. Most psychotic bosses deny they have emotional problems, and even if they admit there is a problem, they're reluctant to reach out for help. So they continue to do what they've always done: wreak havoc on everyone around them—family, friends, and coworkers who must swallow their madness for 40 hours a week.

3. NEUROTIC BOSSES

Psychotic bosses are the worst bosses to cope with. The good news is their numbers pale in comparison to the legions of neurotic bosses out there. It's safe to say that every company has its fair share of neurotic bosses. The bigger the company, the more you'll find. They come in all shapes and sizes. A few of the common types that I've pinpointed follow.

Low Self-Esteem/Insecure Bosses.   Their body language gives them away. The low self-esteem boss would never cut it as a marine. Marines are brainwashed to think they're the best. Once they complete grueling basic training, they look like they've been cut from the same mold. They're perfect physical specimens, strong and tough, every inch of their body reeking confidence. Like the ads say, these individuals are "lean, mean, fighting machines." Our low self-esteem bosses are just the opposite. As kids they were 90-pound geeks who were used as punching bags by the school's tough guys. Sadly, as adults they never got beyond that lowly status. Nobody is beating them up anymore, yet they're always worried that someone might try.

It's no wonder they can't walk with their backs straight and their eyes locked dead ahead. Instead, they're hunched over with their eyes downcast. The very thought of making eye contact triggers a clammy sweat. The expressions on their faces are equally pathetic. Those sad eyes look like the eyes of a dog whose master just gave him away. Their vibrations say, "Praise me! Praise me!" Unlike vicious sadistic bosses who drool about how they can push their subordinates to the brink of suicide, low self-esteem bosses hardly think about their subordinates. Instead, they're fixated on their own miserable plight. They're so obsessed with pleasing their bosses and keeping them at bay that they hardly know what's going on in their own camp. It's only when things go wrong that their tempers flare. It's not so much that mistakes are made, but rather they fear looking bad in their boss's eyes.

I've heard few serious complaints about low self-esteem bosses. They're more a source of amusement than worry. The plus is they're easy to get on with. Praise them and do your job and you'll have no problems. All they care about is getting the work done and avoiding problems. If you're looking to score points, show them how to score with their boss and you've got a friend for life or, more accurately, for as long as you're working at that company.

Paranoid (Fraidy-Cat) Bosses.   A close cousin to the insecure, low self-esteem boss is the paranoid or fraidy-cat boss. These bosses have taken insecurity to the level the shrinks call paranoia. While low self-esteem bosses agonize over pleasing their bosses, paranoid bosses spend most of their waking hours wondering when they're going to be fired. It's a miracle they get any work done at all. Paranoid bosses live in a world made up of plots, secret conversations, and meetings all focused on ousting them from their job.

A secretary working in a mid-size North Carolina textile company describes an incident highlighting her boss's paranoia:

> She was paranoid from the moment she was promoted to department head 5 years ago. You'd think she would have gained some confidence over the years, but she hasn't changed a bit. One day, a friend of mine was sitting on the stairs outside my office drinking a container of coffee and smoking a cigarette when my boss ambled up the stairs. No sooner did my friend see my boss than she lowered her voice and spun around a little so she was facing me. Those innocent moves wrecked my boss's day. By 4 p.m. that same day, my boss couldn't contain herself any longer. She called me into her office, closed the door, and politely asked me to have a seat. Then she told me what was bothering her:

> "Betty, I noticed you and Jenny were having a heated conversation when I came in late this morning. As soon as she saw me she lowered her voice, and it looked like she blushed and changed the conversation. Do you know something I should know, Betty? Is there any scuttlebutt about Jenny's boss? I know she's had her eye on my job for as long as I can remember. I've always been straight with you, Betty. You owe it to me to let me know what's going on. Is there a plot to get rid of me? I wouldn't put anything past Ann Hamhock. She's quite a number. She'd take a contract out on her own mother if she was guaranteed a big promotion. So level with me, okay?"

> If I hadn't been through similar situations before, I would easily laugh at my boss's reaction. But there was nothing funny about it. I looked her straight in the eye and told her she was wrong. I explained that my friend was not talking about my boss or her

boss, but about a mutual friend, another worker, who is going out with one of the company's fast-track MBAs. I told my boss that my friend lowered her voice because no one is supposed to know about the affair. And I hoped that she would keep it a secret. I also told her she was mistaken about my friend blushing. As soon as I explained the situation, it seemed like a huge load had been lifted from her back. There was no conspiracy afoot, and she wasn't about to be ousted from her job. When I finished, you could see the relief in her eyes. It was as if she could go about living worry-free until she picks up another false cue triggering her paranoia.

Thousands of other paranoid bosses resemble this woman. What's fascinating is that it doesn't take much for them to spin incredible paranoid webs. What they don't see or hear they make up. As they see it, the world is out to get them. Similarly fascinating is their warped sense of their own importance. Their entire world revolves around themselves, especially at work. Many are only big fish in little ponds, yet they see themselves as far more powerful than they actually are.

Just as low self-esteem bosses need constant praise and bolstering from subordinates, paranoid bosses need constant reassurance that no one is out to get them. It can be likened to frightened children who are fearful that demons will overtake them in their sleep. Diligent parents quell their fears by telling them demons don't exist. Paranoid bosses have to be reassured in the same way.

Crisis-Driven Bosses.   We've all had a few of these bosses. Always panic-stricken, they have a knack for making it seem like Armageddon is just around the corner. If things aren't done immediately, the company will collapse and the world will end. However, there are seldom any real emergencies. The crises are created by the bosses themselves, typically because they're disorganized and don't have a clue about what's happening around them. Most of these finger-on-the-panic-button bosses are saved by their subordinates who scratch their heads wondering how their bosses ever got their positions. The boss's saviors can be likened to children who find themselves in the unfortunate—and uncomfortable—role of having to care for their parents. Typically, workers feel sorry for these incompetent bosses, but more practically, they continue to cover for them in order to milk the situation for all it's worth.

Many veteran workers who report to crisis bosses have learned to control the situation masterfully, so they're actually running the show. Since the boss doesn't have a clue about what's actually happening, they spin elaborate webs of intrigue, all the while taking 2-hour lunches, leaving early, and even randomly taking days off whenever the mood strikes them. Some cunning employees manipulate their bosses to the point where they're like puppets on a string. At its worst, it's reminiscent of the 1963 British thriller *The Servant,* where a cunning servant actually takes over his master's house and controls his life. More commonly, clever employees use the crisis boss to create an office utopia. How long it continues often depends on how long they can pull the wool over their boss's eyes and still get the work done. Typically, the game can't be sustained forever. Sooner or later, the boss's supervisor gets wise to the scam. Then all hell breaks loose. You can just imagine what happens next.

Compulsive-Obsessive Bosses.   Last but not least is the compulsive-obsessive variety. Most are easy enough to get along with, although they can make everyone around them as nuts as they are. While the two types differ, both tend to let their neuroses get in the way and slow them down. They too depend on loyal subordinates to keep the work moving. The difference between compulsive and obsessive bosses lies in the way they manifest their neuroses. *Webster's New Collegiate Dictionary* defines an obsession as a "persistent disturbing preoccupation with an often unreasonable idea or feeling." For example, assume the boss is fixated on the idea that his boss is constantly watching him, waiting for him to screw up so he can get rid of him. As a result, the obsessive boss makes it a point to always be on his best behavior when his boss is in shouting distance. Or say the boss is consumed by the notion that a competitor will usurp the market with a competing product. She fails to distinguish between observing the competition and obsessing about it to the exclusion of everything else.

Compulsive bosses, on the other hand, get caught up in irrational acts or insignificant details above everything else. Imagine reporting to Felix Unger and you've got an accurate picture of a compulsive boss.

A Chicago copywriter describes a compulsive boss she had to endure:

> She was talented and smart, but inevitably she always got in her own way. No matter what the project, she got caught up in details that slowed down the project. In advertising, that trait could be deadly because you're always fighting the clock. The client is paying to receive a project on a certain date. If we fail to do that, we're in big trouble. If we don't have a good excuse, we face losing the account. On one project, for example, she became consumed with the graphics on a print ad. No one disputes the fact that the look of a print ad is critical. But it's only 50 percent of the project. The remaining 50 percent is the copy or the words that sell the product. Where she should have spent equal time agonizing over every word of the copy, she swept it under the table and relegated the responsibility to an underling incapable of making good decisions. That was the way she did everything. She often got hooked on trivial details. But to her compulsive mind, they were more important than anything else. Her priorities were totally off, but trying to change her mind was like spitting in the wind.

4. INCOMPETENT BOSSES

One of the most infuriating of bad boss categories, incompetents incur well-deserved hatred among their subordinates. To the outside world, they seem like they know what they're doing. But to their employees, they're a joke, and often a sad one when you consider they're paid anywhere from two to ten times more than the workers beneath them. As I explained last chapter, it's easy to understand how incompetent bosses get their jobs. Whether it's nepotism, politics, or special abilities that propelled them to a supervisory job, it's little consolation to the hardworking people forced to kowtow to their incompetence.

Incompetent bosses attempt to hide their weaknesses in the following ways:

- *Buck-passing.*   Some incompetent bosses are masterful at finding the most competent person to complete a task. No sooner does a killer project surface than they pass the buck to someone who can execute it perfectly. It's an automatic act for veteran buck-passers.

- *Taking credit for subordinates' work.*   If passing the buck isn't offensive enough, incompetent bosses unashamedly take credit for work performed by skilled subordinates. And they do so with as much fanfare as possible so their boss thinks they're heroes. If it's an important project worth thousands, even millions, of dollars, the incompetent boss often walks away with a hefty bonus, a week in Hawaii, or a similar reward.

- *Absent without leave.*   It's not uncommon for incompetent bosses who have their act down pat to disappear for a couple of days whenever the mood strikes them. They arbitrarily abandon their command knowing their worker gnomes will run the fort, quelling any fires that might start. These incompetent bosses are useless even when they're in the office. Unfortunately, their workers are also painfully aware of this reality.

Equally astonishing is how long many incompetent bosses manage to pull the wool over their superiors' eyes. Many clever high-ranking corporate executives have done so for an entire career, which is no small feat. They strategically maneuvered their way to power positions as skillfully as world-class chess players. Imagine what they could have achieved if they were actually competent at their jobs.

5. DECEPTIVE BOSSES

Many deceptive bosses are fast-track career types who would do almost anything short of selling their kids for a big promotion. Here are the four most common deceptive bosses.

Manipulative Bosses. The manipulative boss is as slippery as an eel when it comes to getting his or her way. They'll cleverly juggle thoughts or events so they get exactly what they want. It doesn't matter whether they're right or wrong; they're so good at manipulating people that they'll have subordinates apologizing for something they never even did.

Hypocritical Bosses. Underlings never know what to expect from a hypocritical boss. They're as unpredictable as the weather. Their game strategy is "confuse and attack." They'll say one thing and then spin on their heels and do the opposite. Their employees never know where they stand. Their stock and trade is the double deal, which is aimed at making themselves look good. They'll put two workers on an important project, promising each a bonus, raise, or promotion, with no intention of giving both a carrot. The goal is to take the best project, reward the creator, and then disregard promises made to the worker turning in the losing project. Employees working for hypocritical bosses are primed for double-dealings and take it in stride.

Con Artists. A close relative to the hypocrites are con artist bosses who use charm as a weapon. They're smooth as silk and artfully seductive when it comes to getting employees to do almost anything they ask. The motive behind every request or order is furthering their own career. To avoid dissension in the ranks, they'll toss their legions an occasional bone, such as a dinner or a few days off. But the biggest rewards are taken by the boss who has conned his or her superiors as well.

Cutthroats. The worst of the deceptive bosses is the cutthroat. The deceptive bosses just described are bad, but cutthroat bosses can be outright vicious. Employees must be constantly on their guard, ready to fend off attacks at a moment's notice. Cutthroat bosses will use any trick or ploy to get what they want. And if their boss is breathing down their neck, watch out! They'll yell, scream, curse, and bully their employees into turning out an inhuman output. Cutthroat bosses are impostors lacking all human frailties. It's no wonder that turnover in their departments often hits staggering levels. Employees desperate to hold on to their paychecks endure their taunts and insults only until they find a better job. Then they're history. It's easy to understand why workers who've endured cutthroat bosses often quit without giving 2-weeks notice. They deem it a piddling yet well-earned revenge. Can you blame them?

6. REPULSIVE BOSSES

Finally, an amazing number of bosses have hideous personal habits. I worked for one tough old editor who fit the bill perfectly. We called him "The Chimney" because he couldn't quit smoking and he inflicted his bad habit on everyone around him. The man smoked anything he could light. He'd chain-smoke a pack of cigarettes and then switch off to a cigar or pipe. At the end of the day, his oversized ashtray was filled to the brim with butts, squashed stogies, and mounds of pipe tobacco. You'd think the stench would bother him, but he hardly noticed it. Worse yet, he became furious when workers balked at holding meetings in his office. Instead, he made staff members suffer for 2 or 3 hours while his office filled with smoke. During one meeting, one outspoken editor asked if he would refrain from smoking until the meeting was over because it bothered him. He was promptly told that he was a wimp and a disgrace to the newspaper industry. His exact words: "You should work in a laboratory so you could be in a safe, protected environment. Or maybe you ought to be wearing one of those white protective suits so germs can't reach you. You're certainly not cut out to be around human beings." He continued insulting the poor man until he ran out of things to say.

Then, there are bosses who go several days without changing their clothes or shaving. An accountant working for a mid-size food company describes his workaholic boss:

> When we were in the middle of a new product campaign, the boss would literally work around the clock. He was afraid to go home

for fear of missing something. Sometimes his office turned into a combination home and command center for 2 weeks straight. He'd work 18 hours a day and then flop down on his sofa and catch some sleep before starting again. Four days into his workaholic routine and the man looked like a homeless beggar, not a millionaire entrepreneur with two homes, three cars, and a boat. He was unshaven, and his clothes were wrinkled and stained. The worst part is the man smelled from not bathing. We had to endure his repulsive habits. We couldn't tell the boss to go home and shower because he was making everyone around him sick. For all the obvious reasons, we never mustered the courage to be brutally honest.

What do you think of that impressive lineup of bad bosses? You probably never realized there were so many different types out there spewing confusion, incompetence, and venom. But the good news is that most bosses are not half as bad as the ones that have been described. Wouldn't it be liberating to discover that the majority of bosses are human beings just like us? That sounds like a shocking revelation, but the next chapter will prove it to you.

YOUR BOSS IS JUST ANOTHER PERSON HOLDING DOWN A JOB

Meet the Mythical Perfect Boss

Now that you've met some bosses from hell, it's time to get serious and take a critical look at some of the bosses you've had. Don't panic. I know you can do it cold turkey. I guarantee you'll get through it in one piece.

First, we're going to draw a portrait of the mythical perfect boss. Then we'll rock on and look at some of the wonderful bosses you've had.

"GOD, WHY CAN'T YOU GIVE ME A PERFECT BOSS?"

Color Me a Perfect Boss

Who knows where fantasies come from? Movies? Books? How about from conversations? As for fantasies about perfect bosses, maybe a relative told you how much she loved her job because she was encouraged to do her own thing. You thought since she had a great boss you would also. Because of her positive experience, you immediately concluded that a good boss is the key to a great job.

Let's conjure an image of the storybook boss you've always dreamed of having. I asked a small group of people to describe the perfect boss. Interestingly, each one cited similar traits and personality styles. Rather than summarize each one, I put them together to form a composite picture of the perfect boss. Here's what he/she looks like:

- Easy to look up to and emulate.
- Stands out in a crowd.
- Has the bearing and attitude of a leader.
- Takes good care of himself/herself.
- Meticulous about dress and personal habits.
- Example and mentor to others.
- First one to arrive in the morning and the last to leave at night.
- Encourages teamwork and does not play favorites.
- Door is open to everyone.
- Can handle pressure.
- Doesn't take problems out on the staff.
- Mobilizes everyone to get the work done.
- Delivers criticism in a positive way.
- Never raises his or her voice to staff members.
- Gives criticism constructively and in private so staffers don't feel like they're being publicly reamed.
- Meetings are short and productive. Rather than use them as a vehicle to exert power or crucify the staff, he or she turns them into serious brainstorming sessions where everyone leaves motivated.
- Recognizes, appreciates, and rewards hard work.
- Makes you want to do your best because it will pay off in something positive, be it a bonus, raise, promotion, or just a pat on the back and nice word.

- Encourages talent and creativity. It's a pleasure to come to work in the morning.

Summing it up in one sentence: The perfect boss is a born leader, amateur psychologist, and team coach all rolled into one package. Better yet, such an individual is as close to a god as anyone is going to get.

Wow! Here comes the big question: Have you ever been able to heap all those adjectives on any of the bosses you've had? I haven't. But it sure sounds good. Wouldn't you love to meet this person?

What are your chances of having a perfect boss? Conservatively, the odds are worse than winning the lottery. So why concern ourselves with perfect bosses? Perfection is a myth, which means there is no such thing as a perfect anything, be it bosses, employees, friends, mates, pets, you name it.

Now let's blow the myth to smithereens by looking at some of the bosses we've had.

BOSS HISTORY

Here's a sobering blast-from-the-past exercise guaranteed to stir up unpleasant memories. Look at some of the bosses you've had. Depending on your age and the number of bosses you've had to endure, this could keep you busy for the next year of your life. Don't be uptight about admitting a boss put you in therapy. You're not alone. Some therapists owe at least 40 percent of their income to bosses.

The goal is not to look at every boss you've had but to the few memorable ones that left an indelible impression. Most people I've spoken to remember their first boss. If they were lucky, it was a good experience that set the tone for the rest of their career. But whether he or she is your first or last, don't rush through the exercise. Give it time and thought. I guarantee you'll learn a lot.

Once you have your bosses picked out, answer these questions:

1. What was your first impression of this person?
2. What did you like about him or her?
3. What didn't you like about him or her?
4. Did you have anything in common?
5. Did you make a connection with this person?
6. Did you learn anything from this person?

Three examples of boss histories follow. We'll lead off with a first impression from an advertising copywriter from Des Moines, Iowa, followed by a social worker from Los Angeles, California, and finally a mechanical engineer from Kansas City, Missouri.

Note on First Jobs.   The world is new and startling to a newborn baby. Everything around the newborn—people, places, and things—has a profound effect. So say the Freudians. It's the same thing with first jobs. If the initial job experience is positive—you like the job, boss, and coworkers—you expect all the jobs that follow to be positive as well. First jobs set the stage and mood for your career. Conversely, if the first experience was a brief detour into madness, you've been traumatized and expect subsequent jobs to be equally horrendous.

No matter what kind of first job experience you have, count on deprogramming yourself the minute you leave it. Each job means starting over by building new relationships. The tough part is getting an accurate reading on your boss before you take a job. Why walk into a battle zone if you can avoid it? More on that later. Now, a first job impression.

COPYWRITER

I considered myself fortunate. Unlike many of my classmates, I landed a job in a mid-size advertising agency 2 months after I graduated college. A couple of my friends didn't find jobs until 8 to 10 months later. I felt like I was on top of the world. Naturally, I was excited. This was my christening into the world of work. Like any young person starting out, I entertained rich fantasies about what that first job would be like.

I was nervous that first day. I hadn't met my boss because there had been a recent reorganization. The decision to hire me was made by human resources and the senior vice president in charge of creative services. I was taken aback when we met on the first Monday I reported to work. My boss was maybe 5 years older than me. I expected someone older and more experienced. I wasn't thrilled when he told me it was his second job and his first supervisory position. "Oh, God," I thought, "it is the blind leading the blind." But it wasn't like that at all. He was smart and very sure himself. He also looked great. He was smartly dressed and well groomed. The package was impressive.

I made peace with his age by telling myself that if he could move up the ladder this quickly, then I could too. Yet there was a restlessness and nervousness about him that made me uneasy. While he exuded confidence, he seemed anxious to get the amenities over with and get back to work. I expected him to take me under his wing and spend time with me explaining what to do. But that wasn't the case. There is no handholding in an ad agency. Time is money, and my boss didn't intend to waste precious hours showing me the ropes and boosting my ego. It was more than evident from my first half-hour meeting with the man that he was under pressure. His boss must have been on his back; there were deadlines to meet and clients to please. No time to wet-nurse a junior copywriter.

The writing on the wall was crystal clear. It was sink or swim. I was taken to my little cubicle where I was assigned to another junior copywriter who had been there about a year. She briefed me on the clients I'd be working with and gave me my first writing assignments. That was the last I saw of my boss for about a week. I liked the fact that he was a no-nonsense person who gets right down to work, but I wished he'd have spent more time with me. I wanted him to get to know me a little and hear my ideas. But he was all business and didn't have time for anything that didn't concern an immediate project. After I was there a few months, I began to understand why. The man was up against the wall 10 hours a day. The place was a pressure-cooker and the turnover was incredibly high, which didn't make me feel better. Looking back, I appreciate the fact that my boss spared me the news that most of the junior copywriters never made it to the second year. They either quit because the pressure was so intense or they were fired because their work was inadequate.

I regret not making a connection with this person. Maybe he felt it was better to keep a professional distance. That way, it would be easier dispensing criticism or firing me, perish the thought. I may have been young and inexperienced, but I was intelligent enough to know that it was only a job. It wasn't a life-or-death kind of thing. Whether you were a junior or senior person, we were all vulnerable. It would have made for a better relationship if he had loosened up a bit and come across as more human.

But I learned that when starting a new job you have to be ready to hit the ground running. It's great if you have a lot of guidance, but don't expect it. The faster you can master your job, the better off you are.

WELFARE INVESTIGATOR

Jeanne was the third boss I had. My previous bosses were workaholic dynamos. They were the last word in efficiency. Jeanne was the exact opposite. I was totally thrown off by her. She was bright, articulate, and said all the right things, but when it came to getting work done and making decisions, she was out in left field. In fact, if she had a lot on her plate, she turned into a basket case.

I discovered this fact during my third week on the job when I needed her to sign off on a large monthly outlay for a large family who just migrated from Cuba. Jeanne was a welfare department supervisor in charge of over 500 indigent families spread out all over LA. My job as investigator was to do the initial screening and turn in a report on whether I thought they were eligible for public assistance. I also was responsible for coming up with a budget that met the family needs based on the number of people in the family, their ages, and whether anyone in the family was working. That was tough enough. But I quickly discovered that the real frustration was getting Jeanne, my supervisor, to sign off on the family acceptance and budget. She was indecisive and frightened about making big decisions. If the budget exceeded a certain amount of money, she needed approval from her boss. What's more, her output was supervised on a regular basis by her boss, which nearly drove her to drink. But the real pity was that the 50-odd investigators who did all the fieldwork had to wait in line while she waffled until finally making her decision. I was so frustrated at times that I wanted to sock her. She wasn't a bad person; she was just scared, indecisive, and lacked guts. Meanwhile, she asked constant questions, had us redo budgets, and go back to clients to get additional information. Often, clients suffered because they waited weeks or months before they got their first check. We just tried to do accurate fieldwork so she would approve whatever clients we presented.

Jeanne loved the work and was very knowledgeable, but I realized not everyone is cut out to be a boss. She couldn't take the pressure and responsibility of making constant, sometimes rapid-fire, decisions. There were days when we needed to approve as many as 25 new cases. That was more than she could handle. There were times she was so overwhelmed that the poor woman was brought to a complete standstill. Hindsight allows me to be sympathetic and understanding. But when I was in the middle of all that chaos, I was so frustrated I could scream.

Nevertheless, I look back on the job as a good learning experience. When I realized I couldn't function in that kind of restrictive environment, I moved on. I decided to use the experience as a steppingstone to another job where I could get things done more quickly and not have to contend with an insecure boss.

ENGINEER

John was the sixth boss I had and one of the most memorable for a lot of reasons. I was 42 at the time and felt confident about my abilities and knowledge of the construction industry. I consider myself fortunate that John was my boss. He was certainly no perfect boss, yet he was great for me. I lucked out because we had compatible personalities. John was temperamental, opinionated, and erratic, but one the fairest people I've ever met. He had a built-in sense of justice. By the same token, he was impatient and intolerant and wasn't much for small talk. He loved his work and his job, and that is what I respected most. All he cared about was doing the best job he could, and he expected the same from everyone under him. If you did a good job, he let you know it. But if you screwed up, he didn't hesitate to rake you over the coals. As he saw it, you were there to be productive and to learn. If you couldn't cut it, the message was get out and find another job. Blunt and to the point, I liked the fact that you knew where you stood with this guy.

I realized that the first moment I met him. That first interview told the whole story. Unlike some of the other managers I worked for, who delighted in putting engineers through rambling psychological interviews during which ridiculous questions were asked, John didn't ask me any questions about my feelings on work, people, or the meaning of life. He didn't want to know about my people skills either. He didn't care. All he cared about was whether I could do the job. He figured if I could pull that off, everything else would fall into place. He was right.

John wasn't the kind of boss you went drinking with after work or played golf with on weekends. He drew the line when it came to that kind of stuff. I liked that, too. He was strong, tough, and predictable. While I got on fine with him, some of the other engineers couldn't stand him. They resented him for being standoffish and not giving them enough input and direction. They also didn't like the fact that he was not a handholder. If you were paranoid and insecure, John was not a good boss to have. He didn't care about your personal hang-ups. His philosophy was if you have emotional problems, leave them home. If it doesn't affect your work, I don't want to know about it. John proves that chemistry between people is critical. Did you ever meet a couple and say to yourself, "Wow, they're a weird couple. They are so different, yet they get on perfectly"? That's often the way it is with many a boss. John and I were very different, yet we meshed perfectly at work. I doubt we could ever be friends, yet in a boss-worker relationship, we were perfectly matched. There is no figuring human chemistry.

"YOU MEAN MY BOSS IS ACTUALLY A HUMAN BEING?"

DO YOU THINK YOU CAN DO A BETTER JOB?

That exercise was more fun than you expected. What did raking up memories of past bosses tell you? As shocking as it sounds, you've discovered that your bosses are human beings just like yourself. They have warts and blemishes; they're inconsistent, erratic, and sometimes you feel like tossing them out of a window. Still, you can chalk it all up to human nature.

What better time to take a long sober look at yourself? As shocking as it seems, one day you may become a boss. Ponder that scary thought. What then? What will you bring to the table? Forget about how talented you are. That's the smallest part of the equation. Do you have the right personality traits to be a boss? What about all your neuroses? You say you're high-strung now. With 15 people to supervise, you may be bouncing off walls. Not only will you have your own work to do, you'll also have to monitor the performance of others. You'll have to praise and admonish them, not to mention suffer through the headache job of writing performance reviews once a year. That's the easy part. What about the difficult workers, the folks who act up, get out of line, or just plain snap?

The time will come when you'll have to give someone the heave-ho. You'll call the poor schlep into your office, close the door, look solemn, and tell the quaking worker who's been with the company 35 years that there has been a redeployment of resources and you have no choice but to sever his relationship with the company. How are you going to handle it when this bull of a man breaks down and begs you to reconsider? He tells you he's sinking in debt caring for his sick parents, paying college tuition for his 10 kids, not to mention paying child support from a previous marriage. When he looks at you with big teary eyes and begs you to have some compassion, what will you say?

Needless to say, exchanges like this are not fun. If you hope to succeed as a boss, you'll have to be a master of human interaction. Are you up to the task?

WE'RE IN THIS THING TOGETHER

Food for thought: Boss-subordinate relationships are complex. The mistake most of us make is not taking responsibility for the relationship. Whether they're good or bad, we see bosses as enemies, put on earth to torment us and make our lives miserable. So we cleverly extricate ourselves from the relationship, putting the full burden on the boss. In reality, it's a two-way street, and although you're the subordinate, you're nevertheless a major player. Where would the boss be without you? In fact, you may be more than just another cog in the wheel. You could be one of the company's critical support beams. Maybe you're indispensable. That puts another whole spin on the picture, doesn't it? You've got power and leverage that you weren't aware of.

In short, you need each other. It sounds corny, but in an

almost perfect world, the boss-subordinate relationship is a partnership. When it works, it amounts to a good marriage; when it fails, it can be a disaster.

Advice: Take some responsibility for the relationship. Like the cliché says, "It takes two to tango." This sounds like a repugnant thought, yet it's one theme we will be revisiting repeatedly throughout the book.

Now that we've turned the tables for a few minutes, what better time to say several words in bosses' defense? Maybe you've never thought about it, but it's tough being a boss. How tough is it? Read on.

A LITTLE SYMPATHY FROM THE AUDIENCE, PLEASE

It's Not Easy Being a Boss

Before we move ahead to strategies for coping with all types of bosses, a few words in their defense. So you're having problems with your boss. God knows, you're not alone. But your boss also has a side to this story. It may be hard for you to accept, but bosses have something to say from their perspective. Let's look at their problems, their role in the company, and find out what makes them tick.

We've learned how people become bosses, but did you ever consider that not everyone wants to be a boss? Now there's a shocking revelation. As inconceivable as it may sound, not everyone wants to be on the fast-track and enjoy all the accouterments accompanying power. A surprising number of people are content to live secure quiet lives in the shadows. I've known many of them. A couple of my close friends turned down military commissions. One man had a brilliant military career ahead of him. Before technological whiz kids were pulling down megasalaries, he was tinkering with communication technology. The military knew it. The military brass was set to train him to be a communication analyst and foot his college education at the Massachusetts Institute of Technology. When he completed his education, he'd be guaranteed the rank of captain.

My friend shocked everyone, especially his family, when he turned his back on the whole arrangement. Envisioning a life of responsibility, commitment, and worry, he decided to be a free agent with no long-term ties to a career.

Similarly, on the job front, there are countless examples of talented people who have turned down supervisory positions for all kinds of reasons. Fear often heads the list. Thinking they're incapable of shouldering formidable doses of responsibility, they sidestep potential failure by avoiding it. Others are just lazy and don't want to be burdened with responsibility, long hours, employee headaches, and bosses breathing down their necks. Millions of workers just want to crawl into a cubicle so they can do their jobs, be out the door by 5:10 p.m., and get home to have dinner with their families. They have no aspirations of setting the world on fire. They simply want to be left alone and lead a quiet life.

SEDUCED BY LIFE'S CARROTS

Yet, just as many workers who had no grand aspirations of being bosses simply got caught up in life's drama and found they had no other option but to grab the carrot when it was offered. Many people reach for supervisory jobs for economic reasons. They have mortgages, bills, tuition, and mouths to feed. Some are saddled with family problems, like taking care of a sick parent or spouse.

Jeanne, the welfare supervisor mentioned in the prior chapter, is an excellent example. When her husband had an accident and had to accept disability checks until he recuperated, Jeanne was forced to be the family breadwinner. She took the supervisor's exam, passed it with flying colors, and was promoted to the job 3 months later. If her injured husband hadn't been housebound, she would have been content to continue working as an investigator. She loved fieldwork, especially talking with clients face to face, much more than being tied to her desk okaying budgets and keeping tabs on investigators.

Others become bosses because a loved one, often a spouse, pressured them to do so. Their spouses were far more power hungry than they were. For some, money, power, and perks are heady inducements for climbing the corporate ladder. This is still a fact of life in many towns where entire communities sprouted around a company. Flint, Michigan, home of a once enormous General Motors plant, is a classic example. A decade ago, if you lived in Flint, it was almost certain you worked for GM. The bigger your job, the more status and clout you had within the town. While many ambitious workers were pressured by spouses or family members to conquer supervisory jobs, many others were content taking home a decent hourly wage by working on the assembly line 8 hours a day.

But life has a way of forcing us to make decisions and take on responsibilities we'd never consider under ordinary circumstances. Don't for a minute think all bosses love or even want their jobs. Like many of us, they're victims of circumstance. That's pause for thought.

IT'S A JUNGLE OUT THERE

One last thought about being a boss. It's tough being a boss in any age, but it's particularly hard in the 1990s in the midst of the toughest job market ever. A commonly held myth is that most bosses have job security. That couldn't be further from the truth. Unless they're high up and protected by stock options, golden parachutes, and perks, they're often more vulnerable than the average worker. A boss's good or bad work directly affects the bottom line. If his or her staff fails to produce or if sales take a nosedive, the boss is held accountable. Most bosses have the power to hire and fire, yet their heads are on the chopping block every time they make a bad decision. In a competitive environment like ours, the average boss must cope with more pressure than his or her predecessors. Sure, there are jobs out there, but the good ones are hard to come by. And keeping them is harder still. It's difficult for any worker to slip into a cubicle and become invisible, but it's impossible for most bosses. Keep this in mind as you read further.

WHATTA YOU, SOME KIND OF WIMP?

No One Ever Promised You a Rose Garden

Some of us have a distorted take on the world, and we cannot blame our world-view on just one person. We sail through school with great expectations. Our teachers, folks, and friends told us we were great, and we believed them. They gave us a rah-rah speech about what to expect from the job market. Parents often paint fantasies based upon what they would have liked for themselves, while college career counselors excel at giving advice based upon hearsay. Many of these esteemed career counselors have only worked within the hallowed halls of academia. No wonder we launch our careers with skewed information about the work world.

We venture into the real world all pumped up expecting the seas to part as the world breathlessly awaits our arrival. Boy, are we surprised! Our school's career counselors never told us a real job would be like this. Getting used to hard work is difficult enough, but nobody told us we'd have to deal with bosses who were former executioners and serial killers.

It's time for a reality check and two pieces of precious advice.

CRITICAL ADVICE WORTH MEMORIZING

Tip 1: Make No Assumptions About a Job. That includes everything from company culture to boss and coworkers. It's normal to have expectations and fantasies, but don't be shat-tered if they're not met. The more tuned in you are to the people you work with, the better you'll be able to deal with inconsistencies.

Fact: Workers with a high emotional IQ are more likely to make healthy and speedy adjustments. If you remember your Psychology 101 class, the emotional IQ is a better predictor of success than intellectual IQ. The latter only indicates how good you are with abstract, mathematical, and reading skills. The former predicts how successfully you'll integrate yourself into new situations and get along with people. People with high emotional IQs learn how to read people more accurately. In this competitive world, that translates to a priceless talent. Once you get an accurate reading on a person, you will know how to play that person and position yourself for a successful relationship.

While some of us are blessed with supportive relationships that build high emotional IQs early in life, the rest of us must work at it so we learn how to read the right signals and act accordingly. As any shrink will tell you, the only thing stopping most of us from succeeding is ourselves. That sobering piece of truth made Napoleon Hill, author of the timeless *Think and Grow Rich,* a very wealthy man. When we don't accept it, we blame others. It's a less painful way out.

Tip 2: Be As Tough As Your Boss, or Even Better, Be Tougher Than Your Boss. While this sounds good, it may not apply all the time. If you've learned anything so far, it's that bosses are just like the rest of us. They're imperfect human beings trying to make it in an imperfect world. Some are tough; others are weak. You may not be tougher than your boss, but you're certainly as tough, which is all you need to thrive in most jobs. As you read in Chapter Five, you must become a partner in the relationship rather than a victim. You're a player, and a critical one at that.

Let's take a look at some boss-coping strategies.

THE DANGERS OF DOING NOTHING

Solution One: "I'll crawl into a corner and just take it."

Most of us cope with difficult bosses by doing nothing. The most common reasons for doing nothing are fear and laziness, sometimes a combination of both. Fear of the unknown prompts us to hang back and let life run its course. Some justify inertia by taking a fatalistic stance, "Maybe this is the way it's supposed to be. No one said life is easy." My favorite excuse is, "What's the use in complaining? It only gets you nowhere." The attitude is, "Why rock the boat? I had better just shut up and grin and bear it. If I open my mouth, I'm bound to get into trouble."

But organizational psychologists warn against doing nothing. Mardy Grothe and Peter Wylie, authors of *Problem Bosses* (Facts on File), say that doing nothing almost always leads to nowhere. In most cases, it's self-defeating.

HOW PEOPLE DO NOTHING

According to Grothe and Wylie, doing nothing takes one of the following four forms.

1. COMPLAINING AND COMMISERATING

Although everyone complains and commiserates at times, this strategy will ultimately fail you. Complainers whine and bitch about their bosses to anyone who'll listen. They'll spend hours on the phone complaining to coworkers about their horrible boss. When they get home, they'll continue the conversation with spouses and even their children. Some will even complain to their dogs. Still other complainers are so desperate for a sympathetic ear that they'll talk to strangers at bars and bus stations.

All in all, complaining achieves nothing. At best, it offers only temporary relief. The worst part is that it usually alienates people, especially friends and family. Who wants to listen to someone constantly complaining about the same thing? Once in a while it's okay, but when it's incessant, you want to run the other way. Imagine if your spouse began complaining as soon as he or she walked in the door every night. "You won't believe what Carla did today. I've had it. I can't take it anymore. I'm being pushed to the limit. She was really over the top this time. You know the report I spent 3 weeks preparing? Well, she ripped it to shreds and said I did a terrible job. Then she made me rework more than half of it. Can you believe that? I swear to you, Sam, nothing was wrong with the report. She was just being the witch she always is. She has nothing better to do than make everyone else miserable...."

Listening to tirades such as this every day can be grounds for divorce. How far can love's boundaries be pushed?

Besides alienating the people close to you, complaining can blow up in your face if you're not careful. One day, a chronic complainer will make a big mistake and complain to the wrong person, such as a spy, a political maneuverer, or a friend of a friend of the boss. Once the you-know-what hits the proverbial fan, watch out! If the complainer is not fired, his or her life will suddenly turn far worse than before the boss heard about the kvetching.

On the other hand, commiserating, although not as annoying as complaining, achieves the same dismal results. We're all guilty of commiserating. Why, it's practically a national pastime. At any given minute, Americans can be found sitting over lunch, dinner, or having drinks and commiserating about a boss they detest. Millions of hours are spent trading horror stories about dysfunctional bosses.

Not long ago, I was at a popular journalists' bar in Manhattan and I overheard this conversation between two reporters, whom we'll call Sal and Mike.

SAL: Ya heard what John pulled yesterday afternoon just 2 hours before deadline?

MIKE: I sure did. Give the guy an A+ for consistency. If he didn't act like the consummate jerk everyone knows he is, I'd be shocked.

SAL: But how much can a sane person take? I worked my tail off on the story about the shooting in the Bronx, but he wasn't satisfied with the one source who would talk on record. It didn't matter to the nitwit that I had two excellent sources who didn't want to be identified. In fact, John knows who they are and can vouch for their reliability. Nevertheless, at the 11th hour, I had to dredge up another source who'd also go on record. Thankfully, I made deadline just in the nick of time.

MIKE: He pulls that same stuff with everyone. He did it to me last month. Everyone knows he's gutless. If he wasn't a close friend of Salmaggi [the managing editor], he wouldn't have a job.

SAL: You're right on the money, Mikey. He's a gutless wonder who's afraid of his own shadow. Any other seasoned editor would have the guts to stand by his reporters. But that would mean taking a chance.

MIKE: One day he'll get his. He'll screw up and will be out on his butt looking for a reporter's job.

SAL: I'll give him a week on the street before he starts looking to change careers.

MIKE: Amen! Let's have another round on that one, brother.

I'm sure you can recall similar conversations you've heard or participated in. If I look back on the several reporting jobs I've had, I know I can pull up countless exchanges like that one. The good part about them is they have a cathartic effect.

You work off a lot of pent-up energy exchanging horror stories with fellow sufferers. But, like complaining, it goes nowhere.

Once you've engaged in an energetic bout of commiserating, you're back where you started. Your situation remains unchanged.

2. GOOFING OFF

Typically, this pattern of behavior happens slowly. You figure, "Why kill myself for an incompetent jerk who doesn't appreciate me and makes my life miserable?" So you start adding 15 minutes more to your lunch hour whenever you feel like it. In the morning, you barely get in by 9:30 a.m., and at the end of the day, you're darting for the train by 4:50 p.m. On projects, you look for shortcuts and quick solutions. Where you once cared about quality, now you're sole concern is just getting the work completed. When your boss is sick or on a business trip, you take half days off or you don't bother to come in at all.

Not only is this strategy fruitless, but it could also get you in trouble, warn Grothe and Wylie. Unless your boss is a complete moron, sooner or later he or she is going to catch on. In most lines of work, productivity is easy to measure. What will happen come performance appraisal time? Not only will you get a bad review, but you won't even receive a token raise.

3. BEATING YOURSELF UP
(OR TURNING THE PROBLEM INWARD)

Grothe and Wylie call this "internalizing" because you are turning the problem inward, or back on yourself. In this case, the process is more subtle yet still is very destructive. Rather than complaining, commiserating, or slacking off on your job, you turn your anger inward until it eats at you, causing debilitating discomfort in the form of depression, ulcers, and back pain.

Doris, a clothing buyer for a large Detroit department store, wasn't even aware of what she was doing to herself until she sought professional help. Doris loved her job but was petrified of her tyrannical boss who constantly made unreasonable demands upon her. After 3 years of putting up with insults, sarcasm, and bullying, she slowly started to develop back pain. First, she felt pain in her lower back when she sat a certain way. But it rapidly got worse. It developed into sciatica, which brought on shooting pains that ran from her ankles up to her neck. At first, she thought she pulled her back playing tennis, which she played religiously three times a week. She stopped playing for a while, but the pain grew worse. It got so bad she could hardly sit in a chair for more than a brief period. Driving was torture.

She visited various doctors who gave her conflicting diagnoses. One doctor put her on muscle relaxants. Another gave her painkillers. The medicines accomplished nothing other than to make her sleepy or jittery. A chiropractor cracked her back and recommended bed rest. That failed also. As a last resort, she tried acupuncture and massage therapy, both of which produced similar results.

Thankfully, she met a fellow back pain sufferer who had experienced similar symptoms. This person understood what was happening and put her on the right track. She told Doris that the pain was real, yet nothing was physically wrong with her back. It was a psychosomatic pain. Its roots were psychological rather than physiological. In short, it was all in her head. And the only way to deal with it was through psychotherapy. Doris was told she'd likely reject this explanation initially. But when she was ready to accept and tackle the problem, she could work with a psychotherapist specializing in psychosomatic disorders.

True to form, Doris at first told her friend to get a lobotomy. But she came around mighty fast. Hardly 2 weeks later, the pain was so excruciating that Doris could barely sleep at night. This is when she agreed to put herself into therapy. At last, Doris was dealing with the source of the problem. It was not a problem with her back, but rather with her boss. Instead of facing up to the problem, she had internalized it, taking the form of psychosomatic back pain. When she totally understood the cause of her problem, the back pain rapidly disappeared. Her next step was dealing with the real problem, her boss.

Remember: Internalizing is a fruitless method of doing nothing that can cause serious mental and physical discomfort.

4. ESCAPING

Lastly, many workers resort to drugs and alcohol as a way of escaping a difficult boss. Many people don't admit it until their work has deteriorated to a dangerous level or they're on the brink of being fired.

Donald's story is a classic example. Donald was happily employed by a Chicago beverage company as chief accountant for 20 years when his job was suddenly being threatened. When he had started working for the family-run company, there were 30 employees. But over a 20-year period, the company grew to the point where it employed 200 people.

Two years ago, the president hired a CFO (chief financial officer) to oversee the company's books. This is when the winds shifted for Donald. There was no way he could have anticipated or prepared for the change. Ten years his junior, the CFO was a rigid by-the-book bureaucrat with an MBA from the Harvard Business School. In the process of overhauling the company's books, he made Donald's life miserable. First he blamed Donald for the company's ancient method of monitoring finances. Then he burdened him with enough work for three accountants. Worse yet, he was a bit of a sadist, too. Knowing that Donald usually left work at 5:30 p.m. every day to catch a 6:10 p.m. train home, he made a point of calling him into his office at 5:20 p.m., just as he was shoving papers in his attaché case and cleaning up his desk. Then he'd talk to Donald for 40 minutes, piling on work and telling him what he had to do tomorrow. He did this at least three, sometimes four, times a week. By the time Donald got to the train station, he had already missed two trains.

After almost a month of constant stress, Donald couldn't take it anymore and started drinking during lunch. At first, it was just a beer or two with a couple of coworkers. But he quickly discovered that he liked the effect the alcohol had on him. It helped relieve his tension and it made the rest of the afternoon bearable. But after a while, a couple of beers didn't do it anymore. He started drinking scotch. When things were really getting insufferable, he'd consume one scotch followed by two martinis. Miraculously, he still managed to function.

Every time his boss made him miss his train, Donald would promptly march into the tavern in the train station and have a couple of drinks. He kept this up for about 6 months until his work was deteriorating, his health was failing, and his marriage was shaky. He joined Alcoholics Anonymous and started to put the wheels in motion to find another job. It was no small feat considering he was preparing to leave the only job he had ever held.

Alcohol and drugs are common escape valves for workers in many difficult jobs, but especially those in high-stress ones. Drowning your sorrows in alcohol or drugs brings short-term relief when dealing with fierce deadlines, highly exacting work, and a loathsome boss.

Janet, marketing director at a Massachusetts publishing company, religiously smoked a joint during her 45-minute drive home every day. It was the only way she knew how to relieve her job stress and forget about her troubled boss, who made her life miserable.

However, all the pot she had been smoking eventually caught up with her. While driving home one day, the sky suddenly opened up and she found herself navigating through a dangerous rainstorm with little visibility. Unaware that she was careening down the highway at 90 miles an hour, she saw the car in front of her suddenly swerve to avoid a stalled car in the middle lane.

Janet, who was halfway through her joint, managed to jam on her brakes but nevertheless smashed into the car ahead. Thankfully, no one was seriously hurt. But the incident left its mark. Janet realized she could have killed someone, not to mention herself. She never smoked pot again, and she began looking for a healthy solution to her problem.

WHEN DOING NOTHING MAKES SENSE

Yet, at times, doing nothing is a sound strategy. Grothe and Wylie mention the following classic situations: when either you or your boss plans to retire, quit, or transfer to another job.

Imagine you've been with a company for 25 years. Through a merger or consolidation, you've inherited a boss from hell. That's the bad news. The good news is you're only 8 months away from retirement, which equates to leaving the company with a full pension, handsome severance package, and lots of accolades. Blowing your cool by getting on your boss's bad side could get you fired and disqualify you from your full severance package.

Or perhaps you're biding your time because there's a better job in the wings. Why make a scene and create bad blood when your problem is almost resolved by itself?

If the situation is reversed and your boss is about to retire or take a new job, it's the same story. Just grin and bear it until the bane of your workday existence makes his or her final exit. Even if you have to wait 10 months, think about how wonderful coming to work will be when you no longer have to deal with this dreadful boss. That thought alone should tide you over.

One worker described the feeling of waiting for his boss to take another job as waiting to be released from prison. He equated workplace freedom with his boss's departure. But what if he gets a boss who's worse than his prior boss? I'm sure he never considered that frightening possibility.

TUNING OUT
YOUR BOSS

Solution Two: "The heck with my boss. I'm just going to concentrate on my job."

You've often heard, "I'm not going to let my boss stand in the way of my career goals." That's what you say to yourself when you're intent on tuning out your boss and not letting him or her get to you.

This is the essence of a strategy touted by Lyle Sussman, University of Louisville management professor and author of *What to Say to Get What You Want* (Addison-Wesley). Sussman says the focus should be on your work. The goals of this strategy are:

- To put personalities aside.
- To create a legacy for your future work.
- To turn your boss into an irrelevant issue.
- To focus on what you are being paid to do.

Sussman's advice: You will always benefit by being involved in a winning project.

If nothing else, his advice sounds good. But how can you pull it off? Let's find out. Sussman's advice works in two situations:

1. If you're strong-minded and can block out interference.
2. If your boss allows you to concentrate on your work.

BEING A TOUGH-SKINNED PERSON

Let's start with the first one. It takes a tough-skinned person with a strong ego to block out his or her surroundings and concentrate on work. In effect, it's like putting on psychological blinders. These are the individuals who forced themselves to study while friends partied all night long or who prepared for a calculus exam while roommates blasted loud music. It takes self-confidence, drive, hard work, and unbelievable discipline. Most of us are not that strong. In the face of peer pressure, we go with the tides for fear of making waves.

A strong-willed person has the maturity and strength to first size up her work situation and then concentrate on the job at hand. She'll say to herself, "Ted is an incompetent bungler who doesn't know what he's doing. He dawdles and has a tough time making decisions. That's his problem, not mine. I'm not going to let him stand in my way of doing exemplary work."

Harold, a promotion manager for a national cable company, reported to a cocky boss who always had to have his way. He was a hands-in-every-pot kind of boss. Within his first weeks on the job, Harold sized up the man and made an important observation: His boss was no threat to his career. From that point on, he thought of himself as an actor on a stage with the power to control his audience by turning in a brilliant performance. Harold's one-person audience was his boss.

His job turned into a complex game, but it was a very serious one that he intended to win. He viewed his boss as a given who is only technically in the power seat. He realized that if he tuned out his boss, he'd have clear sailing. It amounted to sound advice worth heeding. It may sound cold and calculating, but Harold managed to dehumanize his boss. As soon as he realized that he was no threat to him, his boss became a nonperson. He became a cyborg that just happened to resemble a human being.

Advice: Take advantage of situations you can control by climbing into the power position. Often, who actually controls a situation is a moot point. Your boss is technically the senior person and decision maker earning a lot more money. But no one says you can't control your boss by cleverly manipulating the situation to be in your favor. Harold did it, and millions of others are quietly doing it every day. Yes, it's manipulation. But what's wrong with that if you're getting what you want and nobody is getting hurt?

Employees controlling their bosses again remind me of the classic 1963 British thriller *The Servant*. It's so similar to employee-boss relationships that I urge you to watch it and study the dynamics between servant Dirk Bogarde and employer James Fox. The intricate psychodynamics in the film elevate it to cult classic status. I'm not suggesting you use the corrupt and decadent Bogarde character as a role model. But it's fascinating how one person in a seemingly inferior position can become the master and subtly dominate and control the relationship. This situation is very possible in the workplace when you have bosses who are no intellectual matches for their employees. As the saying goes, "They're like putty in your hands."

Harold's goal was to further his career, and he didn't care how he did it as long as it didn't put him in jail. Once he sized up his boss, he knew he could control the situation by placating him and giving him what he needed. But not everyone is as lucky as Harold, which brings us to the second situation where Sussman's advice can work.

CONCENTRATING ON YOUR JOB

To concentrate solely on your job, your boss must allow you to do so. Assume there will be a certain amount of interference, but the key is that it won't be so overwhelming or overbearing that you're brought to a complete standstill.

Helen, a securities analyst at a small Philadelphia brokerage house, reported to Martha, a tough, domineering supervisor who was like a powerful fullback blocking her every move. If Helen was more intuitive, she wouldn't have taken the job. The vibes were bad the second they clapped eyes on each other. Martha's angry piercing stare and interrogative manner were off-putting. At the time, Helen made light of it. She was young, inexperienced, and wanted to work for a small brokerage firm where she could build credentials and contacts. Helen disregarded Martha's overbearing manner by saying, "It was only my first impression. Once she gets to know me and discovers I'm a hard worker who wants to do great work, we'll be great friends." But just the opposite happened. Helen went on to do a great job and make a lot of friends, but Martha wasn't one of them. The more friends Helen made and the more she accomplished, the greater the animosity between the two women.

It didn't take Helen long to figure out what the problem was. The two women were complete opposites. Helen was young, pretty, and in the liftoff phase of what promised to be a long and accomplished career. What's more, she started out with the right accouterments. She had graduated from Smith College with honors in the top 10th percentile of her class. Martha, on the other hand, was a dowdy, overweight woman in her late 40s who was forced to quit college after her sophomore year to help support her sick parents. While she was a hard worker, she didn't have the elegant upper-middle-class background that Helen carried with her like a proud mantle. Helen grew up privileged with comfort and luxury. Martha's parents, in contrast, were working class, uneducated, and poor. Since money was always an issue in her home, Martha had been working since she was a teenager.

On the job, Martha started off at the bottom, but advanced quickly. However, she never got beyond a low-level supervisory slot. And that's where she's been for the past 8 years. Her career is stalled, and she realizes that she's not going any further. Management sees her as past her prime. They won't get rid of her because she does her job well, but they're also not going to promote her because plenty of other workers are equally bright, if not brighter, and present a better image. In the corporate world, image and impression weigh heavily into the success equation.

It's obvious that Martha's seething hatred and jealousy will make it impossible for Helen to advance. She'll block her every move. If she encourages Helen and gives her the freedom she deserves, it won't be long before she achieves equal ranking. After that, it's only a matter of time before she'll overtake Martha on the corporate organization chart.

At this point, one can only guess what will happen in the Helen and Martha drama. One thing is certain: As long as Helen reports to Martha, she will never be able to be all she could be in her job. However, things could turn around quickly. Since Helen is an obvious shining star, senior management might step in and whisk her away from her jealous and bitter supervisor. Or Helen could take a better job. I lean toward the former possibility. Tight corporate cultures are like small towns where everyone knows each other's business. Martha is tolerated and respected, but Helen is the clear favorite. She's the thoroughbred horse at the starting gate. Everyone knows it's only a matter of time before she bolts toward the finish line ahead of everyone else.

But don't be discouraged if this solution doesn't work. There will be more ahead.

"MY BOSS IS EVIL AND THAT'S ALL THERE IS TO IT"

Solution Three: Validate your assumptions.

Millions of people believe they're working for the devil incarnate or a Mafia killer in training. They seldom consider that their boss may not be evil or "toxic," as Lyle Sussman, author of *What to Say to Get What You Want,* calls it, but is just incompetent. There's a big difference.

Whether we admit it or not, we all suffer from some degree of paranoia. We imagine confrontations, personality conflicts, and plots and intrigue where none exist. At the top of the list, we're convinced that our boss is a sadist and we're the object of her wrath. If properly embellished, it's the stuff of sitcoms. But that's seldom the case.

Some of us are such hopeless egomaniacs and narcissists that we're unable to see that our boss is just a poor slob trying to keep a job. It's human nature to unconsciously thrust ourselves into the center of every life drama, regardless of whether we deserve a starring role. We see only our own troubles and fail to see that everyone else is in the identical boat. The boss is on everyone's backs. If we knew how to put our angst on hold, we'd find another outlet for our anxiety.

DON'T GIVE BOSSES TOO MUCH CREDIT

THEY'RE NOT THAT SMART

Consider this reality: Your boss may not be evil, just inept or stupid, maybe both. That puts a whole new spin on things, doesn't it? "Never attribute to malice what can be explained by incompetence or lack of interpersonal skills," says Sussman. "Don't arbitrarily assume your boss is out to get you. While bad bosses get branded in our memory, very few bosses are outright toxic."

Solution three is all about understanding and isolating the problem. Once you "validate" your assumptions by exposing them, your boss will stop getting to you. Sussman contends that just understanding the dynamics of the relationship is inspiration enough to concentrate on becoming a shining star.

Start by asking these questions about your boss.

"RATE YOUR BOSS" QUESTIONNAIRE

Answer questions *yes* or *no*. For questions marked with an asterisk, use a scale from 1 to 10, where 10 = excellent, 5 = fair, and 1 = horrendous.

1. As a leader, how would you rank your boss? Does he take charge or wait for others to come up with the bright ideas?*
2. Does your boss inspire confidence?
3. Does he set the tone for and pace of projects?
4. As a decision maker, how do you rank him?*
5. How would you rank him as a coach and motivator?*
6. How does he handle a crisis?
7. Does he thrive or crumble under intense pressure?
8. Where does he stand on the organizational ladder? How does management feel about him?

9. How secure is your boss's job?*

10. As a professional, how would you rate your boss? Is he an ethical and moral person, someone you look up to and admire?*

11. Is he a risk taker who will support a speculative project?

12. Will he stand by a gifted worker who took chances or messed up on a project?

Here are two different sets of answers, both of which shed light on how workers see their bosses. The first is from a clothing salesman in Arkansas; the second is from a telecommunications technician in Kansas.

ANSWERS OF THE CLOTHING SALESMAN

1. Q. As a leader, how would you rank your boss? Does he take charge or wait for others to come up with the bright ideas?*
   A. As a leader, I'd give him a 2 and that's being generous. If we were in combat and I had to fight under him, I'd probably desert. That would be a better alternative to getting myself killed following him. As for bright ideas, he has none. If he didn't have bright people working for him who continually save his ass, he'd be collecting unemployment checks.

2. Q. Does your boss inspire confidence?
   A. He inspires no confidence. I wish he did. All the salespeople think he is a joke. He was promoted to supervisor because he was a good salesperson who simplemindedly captured an entire region himself. So management naturally assumed he'd be a great boss. Were they wrong! With any luck, they'll come to their senses and realize they made a big boo-boo.

3. Q. Does he set the tone for and pace of projects?
   A. He sets no tone. He just shows up every day so he doesn't lose his job. The kicker is he doesn't have to

contribute anything since he gets a percentage of the sales of the entire department. By bringing in great numbers, we make him look good.

4. Q. As a decision maker, how do you rank him?*
   A. I'll be generous and give him a 1.5 as a decision maker. In the course of a year, he's good for a couple of inconsequential decisions, such as where we have our annual sales meeting and what the menu will be at our Christmas dinner. He's good at that. As for real on-the-job-type critical decisions, I can't think of any he has made. Actually, we make the decisions, and he stands by them because he knows he can't make any on his own. He trusts our instincts, which is a frightening reality since this guy is paid a handsome salary to be our leader.

5. Q. How would you rank him as a coach and motivator?*
   A. He's never been a coach or a motivator. On both counts, I'd give him a 1. Both require energy, intelligence, and some drive. But he has none of these attributes. He's learned that he doesn't have to do very much to keep his job and collect his pay. He lets the department kind of run itself and hopes everything will be okay. So far, he's been lucky.

6. Q. How does he handle a crisis?
   A. He doesn't handle crises; we do. The reasons are pretty selfish. If there is some kind of foul-up and we somehow don't turn in the sales figures management expects, we're in trouble because we're in the field getting the sales. He is supposedly monitoring us, but all the salespeople know he's incapable of doing that. He doesn't know how.

7. Q. Does he thrive or crumble under intense pressure?
   A. It's pretty much the same story when it comes to pressure. He neither thrives nor perishes under it. He's impervious to it. Now that's talent. The man has the feelings of an amoeba.

8. Q. Where does he stand on the organizational ladder? How does management feel about him?

   A. There's the rub. He's still employed, so management must like him. I guess he's pulled the wool over their eyes for so long that they actually think he's useful. My boss is a schmoozer and butt-kisser. If the man does one thing well, it's protect himself.

9. Q. How secure is your boss's job?*

   A. Unfortunately, I'd say he's pretty solid with management, which means he's going to be around for a long time. On the security scale, I'd give him an 8+.

10. Q. As a professional, how would you rate your boss? Is he an ethical and moral person, someone you look up to and admire?*

    A. As a professional, I'd give him a 1 and maybe that's too high. As for ethics and morals, I doubt if he knows what the words mean, nor does he care. The man is a survivor who looks after number one first. If you fall into his scenario and strengthen his position, you're needed and therefore are secure.

11. Q. Is he a risk taker who will support a speculative project?

    A. Risk taking is another term that never found its way into his vocabulary. He takes no chances. His philosophy is, "Why take risks if you don't have to?" That's why he has people under him. If anything happens, he makes sure they take the heat.

12. Q. Will he stand by a gifted worker who took chances or messed up on a project?

    A. That depends on what the results were. If someone experiments and tries a new selling strategy or spends an inordinate amount of time on a risky account, he'll make sure his superiors know that he's got a wild card working for him that he doesn't totally support. That way, he protects himself should anything go wrong. If the worker falls on his face, management will know that my boss is on top of the situation. If the worker succeeds, my boss will make sure senior management knew that he stepped in and gave a helping hand. Either way, my boss wins. He gambles on nothing. If it's not a sure bet, he avoids it like the plague.

Analysis: Needless to say, this person has strong feelings about his boss. By the time you reach the second answer, you know that he thinks the man is a nitwit of gargantuan proportions. Filling out this questionnaire has to be a cathartic exercise. It sure beats bellyaching with coworkers over a few beers after work.

Now let's look at some more answers.

ANSWERS OF THE TELECOMMUNICATIONS TECHNICIAN

1. Q. As a leader, how would you rank your boss? Does he take charge or wait for others to come up with the bright ideas?*
   A. On the leadership scale, I'd give my boss a 5+. The problem is he's inconsistent, which has to do with his own insecurities about his standing within the firm.

2. Q. Does your boss inspire confidence?
   A. For the above reason, he doesn't inspire a whole lot of confidence. Often, we're not quite sure where he stands or how he feels, which can be very disorienting.

3. Q. Does he set the tone for and pace of projects?
   A. When the stars are right and he's confident about the outcome, he often sets the pace and tone of projects. Other times, we have to get the ball rolling and initiate things or else nothing gets done.

4. Q. As a decision maker, how do you rank him?*
   A. As a decision maker, I'd give him a 5. Again, his indecisiveness puts him smack in the middle. When he's in control, he can be a dynamo capable of making smart decisions. But when he's unsure, he wavers and the staff must pick up the slack.

5. Q. How would you rank him as a coach and motivator?*
   A. There are times when my boss can be a marvelous coach and motivator. He's a smart person who could be incredible at his job if he had more control over his own destiny. He deserves a 7.

6. Q. How does he handle a crisis?
   A. He handles crises erratically. His own insecurities about his capabilities get in the way sometimes. However, there are times when he's up against the wall yet manages to pull through.

7. Q. Does he thrive or crumble under intense pressure?
   A. For the most part, he rises to the occasion and handles pressure well. In fact, it often takes a killer deadline to bring out the best in the man. That's when he's a pleasure to work with, and you can count on him to stay until the work gets done.

8. Q. Where does he stand on the organizational ladder? How does management feel about him?
   A. He doesn't have a lot of clout in the organizational ladder. One of my boss's big problems is that he doesn't know how to play organizational politics. Management doesn't know quite what to make of the man. They don't know where he stands because he hasn't aligned himself with any faction. That puts him in limbo with no one to back him.

9. Q. How secure is your boss's job?*
   A. Considering the above, my boss's job is not that secure. To make matters worse, he's only been with the company for 3 years, which makes him the low person on the seniority scale. He's vulnerable and he knows it. That probably contributes to making him an indecisive leader. I'd give a 4 rating.

10. Q. As a professional, how would you rate your boss? Is he an ethical and moral person, someone you look up to and admire?*
    A. Here's where I give my boss high marks. As an ethical

and moral professional, I'd give him a solid 9. He's not a backstabber and he sincerely loves what he does. He's a fine technician who's come up through the ranks and can recognize talent in others. While we have problems with his indecisiveness, everyone knows he can be trusted, which is unusual in the corporate world. For these traits, he's to be admired.

11. Q. Is he a risk taker who will support a speculative project?
    A. It depends. Typically, he's less apt to take chances with his own projects, yet I've seen him stand behind workers who invested countless hours on a project with tentative outcomes.

12. Q. Will he stand by a gifted worker who took chances or messed up on a project?
    A. Absolutely. I've seen it happen often. Maybe it's his built-in ethical core that prompts him to help and encourage people under him. On many occasions, I've seen him work until 9 p.m. with a worker who had messed up a project. He feels a sense of responsibility for the people who report to him. I don't think he wants anyone to lose his or her job.

Analysis: This man's answers revealed a whole different feeling. Where the first person demonstrated contempt and hatred for his boss, the telecommunications technician is sympathetic and understanding. While frustrated by his boss's inconsistency, he's taken the time to understand him. It's easy to see that he both admires and feels sorry for the man. He sees him in a precarious juggling act, backing his workers yet unclear of how to assert himself with his fellow managers. What we're getting from this worker is both sympathy and empathy for his boss's tentative position in the firm.

The beauty of this exercise is that it doesn't matter whether you love or loathe your boss. Merely looking at the situation honestly and intelligently is liberating. Uppermost, it accomplishes its goal of validating your assumptions about your boss, just as Sussman suggested.

We're making progress. Slowly but surely, we're getting a clear handle on our boss. This is only the beginning. There are many other strategies ahead. Now that you've validated your assumptions, what do you do with them? One approach is to use your boss as a negative role model. In the next chapter, you'll find out more.

"DO I LOOK LIKE SOME KIND OF MASOCHIST? WHY WOULD ANYONE WANT TO BE LIKE MY BOSS?"

Solution Four: Think of your boss as a negative role model.

Everyone makes a big deal about positive role models. Books have been written on the subject. Experts stress the long-term value of finding someone you can emulate, look up to, and learn from. That's utopia, the view-from-the-sky outlook. Now it's time for an eye-level point of view.

The fact is that often there are few positive role models around. What better example than many of our job situations? Most of us invest countless hours bitching and complaining about how horrible our bosses are, never considering that our bosses could be used as negative role models. It never dawned on us that much can be learned from negative behavior. Rather than spending the next few years just trashing your boss while on your shrink's couch, put him or her under the microscope and learn something. This negative behavior has a positive flip side that can help you better adjust to your position and thus do a bang-up job. How does that sound?

When you think about it, it makes perfect sense. Naturally, you're not going to follow your boss's example. But instead of shrugging off the behavior, learn from it and keep it in mind for future reference. It goes to show that you can learn something from everyone, even the jerks and lunatics of the world.

I urge you to revisit the material in Chapter Three. *Remember:* Anyone can be a boss. The majority of bosses weren't trained for the job. They learned by doing. Unfortunately, you're the victim. So, why not profit from it?

"I NEVER REALIZED IT WOULD BE SO MUCH FUN WATCHING MY BOSS SCREW UP"

CREATING A LOG OF YOUR BOSS'S BEHAVIOR

Once you get started, you'll actually enjoy using your boss as a negative role model. And you'll be surprised that you will learn more than you dreamed possible.

Your goal is to evaluate your boss's behavior critically and extract lessons from it. Here's how you do it. As often as possible, take notes and record your boss's behavior. It would be ideal if you can do this several times throughout the day. However, if your schedule is frantic and you barely have time for a cup of coffee, you'll have to be content to take notes at the end of the day or possibly in the comfort of your home.

It's important to find time for this task. The more information you can record and the more precise you can be, the better you'll be able to critically evaluate your boss's negative behavior.

It's impossible to carve up a day hour-by-hour, so you could do it this way:

Early morning

Midmorning

Noon to 2 p.m.

Midafternoon

Late afternoon
Early evening

For the first few days, simply jot down the behavior patterns. Note the following observations of a veteran salesperson working for an Ohio office supply company.

Week of July 2

Early morning: Lucretia usually arrives at about 8:30 a.m. She walks into her office, barely acknowledges anyone, and closes the door. Five minutes later, she comes out, coffee cup in hand, and heads for our floor's kitchen where the coffee is brewing. She pours herself a cup, heads back into her office, and closes the door behind her. We don't see her again until about 10:30 a.m.

Midmorning: Lucretia emerges from her office to get the regional sales reports from the salespeople. She grabs the sales reports and takes them into her office, closing the door behind her. About 11:30 a.m., she emerges for the morning meeting where our regional managers discuss strategies for increasing sales and breaking into new territories. If sales are down, she criticizes the managers for their poor performance. When sales are up, she says they could be better.

Noon to 2 p.m.: By 12:30 p.m., Lucretia leaves her office, closing her office door behind her. We don't see her again until 2 p.m. Often, she doesn't return until about 2:30 p.m.

You get the idea. About a week or 10 days later, go to the next step and start evaluating your boss's behavior and drawing conclusions next to each observation. For example:

ANALYZING BAD BEHAVIOR

Early morning: Once again, Lucretia is her disgruntled self. She doesn't acknowledge anyone and disappears into her office. One wonders what she does until 10:30 a.m. We interpret the closed door as a warning to stay away. The few times we've knocked on her door to get information, she seemed annoyed, as if we were interrupting something important. However, none of us had any idea of what it could be. Nevertheless, we took the hint and now wait for our leader to emerge. We assume that whatever she is doing is not work-related. She certainly wasn't discreet about that fact either.

Midmorning: Again, Lucretia remains aloof. It almost seems as if she works at being distant. When she first took over the department, we all thought she didn't care for any of us. On closer scrutiny, we concluded that it was a combination of insecurity, paranoia, and outright incompetence.

Noon to 2 p.m.: Again our boss remains scarce, fueling the mystery around her. Lunch hours serve as an opportunity to socialize and also get some work done in a more convivial atmosphere. Yet, Lucretia shies away from any kind of personal contact, almost fearing it like the plague. That told me a lot about her personality and her ineffectiveness as a leader.

There is no point in running through every detail of this worker's entries. But if we were to take some nuggets of information from them, it's clear that the boss is an excellent example of a negative role model.

This worker drew the following conclusions about the boss:

- She has a problem with people, yet makes no effort to communicate.

- Not only does she not reward good work, but she also has no clue how to provide constructive criticism when someone messes up.

- Like so many bad bosses, she denigrates workers in front of their peers like a parent publicly reaming a child. All it does is incur the wrath of her workers.

Summing up, this worker wrote:

Without direction, encouragement, and support, morale in our department is very low. As a result, we find ourselves working not for the company but for ourselves. What could be a career path is just a job and a paycheck. The crowbar in the machinery is our boss. Most of us are biding our time figuring out what we're going to do next. Do we stick it out and try to overcome this major obstacle, transfer to another department, or look for another job? The consensus of opinion is that we deal with it together, try to overcome this roadblock called our boss, and do an excellent job despite her.

You get the idea. After 2 to 3 weeks of observing your boss, you will come away with a wealth of information. You can stop playing organizational psychologist and concentrate on your job, having gained new insight. By then, it will be clear to you that each one of your boss's negative traits is a lesson for what not to do both as a boss and also as a worker who must work harmoniously with others.

There is no such thing as a perfect work setting; yet, it's the responsibility of both management and workers to come as close as possible to that elusive goal. By observing Lucretia, this worker was able to see the effects her behavior had on the staff. As the worker noted, the flip side was that Lucretia's problems and inadequacies brought this worker closer to her coworkers. Intelligent analysis, rather than simply bellyaching and complaining, welded them into a stronger team.

Advice: The process of seeing your boss as a negative role model requires you to step back from the relationship to see it more clearly. In the process, you'll learn a great deal. Chances are you're going to share your knowledge with fellow workers. Hence, a common bond, better teamwork, and camaraderie result. When apathy is replaced by understanding and hope, a new and healthier coping mechanism emerges.

There is real value in using your boss as a negative role model. Let's move on and consider another solution: changing ourselves.

"MAYBE I SHOULD CHANGE"

Solution Five: Consider modifying your behavior so you can work more harmoniously with your boss.

You're probably saying to yourself, "If I see the word 'change' bandied about again, I'm going to have a blood-curdling temper tantrum." I don't blame you. Change has become one of those annoying buzzwords that triggers rage and hostility. Politicians promise to "change" the world, self-help gurus swear it's the foundation for spiritual and intellectual growth, and modern employers insist they want workers who can "change" with the company and keep pace with technology.

You hear so much about change that it almost makes you become a misanthrope and move to the hills of Appalachia. With all this talk about change, you'd think the world would be a better place.

Nevertheless, there are times when it's necessary to talk seriously about change. There are two ways to embrace it. First, you can actually work at changing yourself or, second, act like a chameleon and pretend to change. What do these strategies mean?

In the former, you actually put forth a sincere effort to change yourself. In the latter, you are an actor on a stage who's playing a role. The goal is simply getting through a tough situation by temporarily adopting certain behaviors. Which strategy makes more sense? I know you want me to give you the correct answer, but I can't. It's a personal call. You'll understand why when you have a better idea what both of these strategies mean. First, let's look at the notion of pretending to change.

"I'LL BE ANYTHING YOU WANT ME TO BE—OKAY?"

This is the easiest strategy. It requires no heavy soul-searching, angst, or work. You'll be manipulating a situation to get what you want. Don't be offended by the word "manipulating." We're all manipulative in our own ways, some more than others. Manipulation is a basic survival mechanism. Small children manipulate their parents and siblings to get what they want. They kiss ugly aunts so they give them a quarter to buy candy. They feign sickness and create incredible tall tales to stay home from school or get out of chores. I'm sure you've done some remarkable numbers on friends to turn a situation your way.

So what's repugnant about manipulating our bosses to get what we want? Don't get the wrong idea. I'm not endorsing this strategy. It's up to you to find the best solution. I'm only alleviating any pent-up guilt you might have over the concept.

Advice: This is a short-term, quick-fix strategy which is ideal for dealing with off-the-wall bosses. Consider this scenario: There has been a major shakeup at your company in the form of a takeover, consolidation, or merger. A democratic, fair-minded boss was replaced with a raving tyrant who is instituting blanket changes throughout the company. It's analogous to a tornado heading right at you. What do you do? Be destroyed or protect yourself? Obviously, the latter solution is recommended. You quickly adapt and become the eager-beaver worker who welcomes the tyrannical despot with open arms. You welcome this person by transmitting positive vibes. You make it seem like the new regime is a breath of fresh air and your boss is the Messiah wearing an Armani suit. That's what being a chameleon is all about.

The chameleon strategy is also recommended if you're planning on taking another job. What's the point of working on changing yourself if a better job waits in the wings? If it means sticking it out for 3 to 6 months, some creative play-acting is a painless course of action.

The more difficult path is changing yourself. Let's find out what that entails.

CHANGING YOURSELF—
EASIER SAID THAN DONE

On the surface, it seems that changing yourself makes the most sense. In a mature moment, you say to yourself, "Heck, my boss may be an idiot, but I'm not perfect either. I have a lot to learn. So what do I have to lose by changing? I'll probably be a better worker, maybe even a better human being, for the effort. I'll reap the benefits for the rest of my life."

It sounds great, but let's think about it. The notion of changing yourself seems like a simple enough concept, yet most of us have no idea what's involved. Self-improvement is fashionable. You'd be from another planet if you didn't think change is good. But the truth is that most of us find change intolerable. In fact, the very idea of changing ourselves is so repugnant that we reject it before we ever seriously consider it. The reason is most people don't believe they have to change. They're content with themselves. Defense mechanisms kick into place, and you categorically reject the very idea of changing. The thinking goes something like this: "Change myself! Are you kidding? Why do I have to change? It's my boss that needs to straighten out, not me. She's the one with a serious personality disorder."

Before you give the notion of change serious thought, make sure you actually want to do it. Despite what the self-help snake charmers say, changing yourself ain't easy. It involves hard work.

If you decide to go for it, start by finding out what areas need to be changed. There are four obvious information sources for advice: yourself, family, coworkers, and boss. Let's look at each one.

Yourself. While this is less than an objective source, it is still a good place to start. You're bound to learn something, so get a pencil and paper and list things you'd change to improve the relationship between yourself and the boss. It will be interesting whether your perception of what needs to be done jibes with everyone else's.

Family.   While spouses and close relatives are not physically present at your jobs and they don't see the subtleties of your relationship with your boss, they nevertheless represent a valuable information source. Most people discuss work issues and problems with loved ones. It's practically an automatic response. Your family, especially your spouse, is a release valve for the pressures and frustrations of the job. Unfortunately, spouses often take a good deal of abuse in that area when individuals discharge pent-up anger that should have been leveled at their bosses. If you tell your boss to take a hike, you risk getting fired. Shifting that anger to your spouse risks an equally devastating fate—winding up in divorce court.

At a calm moment, ask your spouse or family members for an opinion on the subject. Find out how they see the situation. What insights and constructive criticism can they offer?

Coworkers.   The most objective source is coworkers. While family members are a potentially good information source, they may be unwilling to be totally candid, especially if the blame rests mostly on your shoulders. They may not want to hurt your feelings or bruise your ego. Coworkers, however, if approached in the right spirit, can be the best source of objective information. But how you approach them and, most of all, your willingness to hear the truth make the difference.

Don't offhandedly corner a coworker at the water cooler and ask what changes he or she suggests. I guarantee that will produce dismal results. All you'll get are platitudes and little truth. If you want constructive insights and objective criticism, some strategy is needed.

First, decide which coworkers you want to approach. The more opinions you gather, the better. But think carefully about whom you want to approach. Ideally, you want people who will level with you rather than just tell you what you want to hear.

Second, once you've identified people who will be honest, schedule a private meeting with each one. The goal is total honesty. The only way you're going to get it is by speaking to each coworker privately. People are more likely to be candid in a one-on-one meeting. If you turn it into a group meeting, the tone will immediately lighten up.

Time and place are also important. The ideal time would be after work when there are no time constraints. Lunch hours can be tense. By the time you actually sit down to talk and get to the serious issues, you're left with barely 30 minutes. Find a quiet bar or coffee shop where you can unwind and talk.

Third, plan the meeting and have an agenda. I heartily recommend going into the meeting with prepared questions and a pad for jotting down notes. It tells the person that you're very serious about getting truthful answers.

Once the stage is carefully set, be prepared for brutal honesty. You might not like what you're going to hear. No matter how smart and enlightened you think you are, no one likes listening to bad news.

The meeting may proceed as follows:

> As you know, Hortense, it's no secret I'm having some serious problems with Edmund. Nothing I do is right. It's really getting me down. After all this time, I thought things would get better, but it seems they're only getting worse. I need you to be honest with me, Hortense. Do you think I'm contributing to the problem? What can I do to ease the tensions and build a productive working relationship?

Now sit back and wait for some surprises. You might not like an answer such as:

> As I see it, Porter, there seems to be a real personality clash between you and Edmund. Your personality styles are totally different. Edmund is tentative, indecisive, and reluctant to take a stand, whereas you know exactly what you want and have no qualms about expressing an opinion. He's timid, shy, and repressed. You're totally out there exuding total confidence. You're ready to take on the world, and he's afraid of it. To sum up, he sees you as a threat.

He's so paranoid and insecure that he probably thinks you're after his job. Every time you express yourself at a meeting and challenge his ideas, he thinks you're being hostile. I know you're attacking the problem, not him, but Edmund doesn't see it that way. He thinks you're out to humiliate him in front of the whole department. That's why he won't acknowledge your observations. Even though you make perfect sense and offer excellent rebuttals, he thinks you were put on earth to make his life miserable.

As for what you can do to mend the rift—you can start by cooling it. It seems that you cannot see the forest from the trees. Put a muzzle on your opinions. You're not going to like this, Porter, but even though you totally disagree with him, keep your opinions to yourself. The only time he feels like a leader is when he is not being challenged by anyone. Why do you think we all muzzle our opinions and let him do his thing? You're the only one who doesn't do that. And you've paid a hefty price for it. As long as he runs the department, your chances of moving up are severely limited. Why do you think Eldridge got a big promotion and you didn't? That was totally ridiculous, and we all knew it. Eldridge has been with the company only 2 years; you've been here 6. But the biggest insult was Eldridge is a jackass and just as incompetent as Edmund. That's precisely why he was bumped up. Edmund likes him because he's stupider than he is. That's quite a feat. You're so wrapped up in your own little world, this probably passed you by.

The best advice I can give you, Porter, is to stay in your office and don't come out. Be seen but not heard. If you're lucky, Edmund will back off and stop harassing you.

If I were Porter, I'd be a little upset after digesting that barrage of honesty. Even though he braced himself for the worst, some of Hortense's candid remarks had to tear at his ego like cutting lashes from a bullwhip. Put yourself in Porter's shoes. How would you react if you had to absorb these brutally honest observations? Food for thought, no?

Your Boss.   Yes, you can take the bull by the horns and confront the source of your angst by putting your cards on the table. But I don't recommend it, especially if you don't have another job in the wings.

Most employees seldom ask their boss such questions,

according to Grothe and Wylie. The reasons are obvious. You could be opening a dangerous Pandora's box. Imagine approaching Edmund and asking him what you might do to change and what advice he offers to build a more productive working relationship. In the privacy of Edmund's office, you might hear something like:

> How do I think you should change? I never thought you'd ask. If you look at yourself in a mirror, you'll see a dysfunctional klutz. If I were you, I'd find a cheap shrink who'll see you five times a week. That's how much you need help. You've got massive personality problems. You don't belong in an organization working closely with people. You're a loose cannon, a misfit. You're the antithesis of a team player. In short you're not cut out for corporate life. What do I suggest? Two words: Career change! Take my advice and hand in your resignation today. Why wait until tomorrow?

Aren't you sorry you asked?

Advice: Only approach your boss if you're ready for fireworks. You could be setting off a powder keg. I exaggerated the foregoing dialogue, but the important point is that many bosses are unapproachable. The fictitious Edmund is one of them. Later on, we'll discuss one-on-one confrontations in greater depth. Managing the meeting requires finesse, self-awareness, and strategic interpersonal skills.

EPIPHANY! MAYBE IT'S NOT WORTH IT

After getting the real story from your family and coworkers, you may decide that it's not worth it to change. This is not to say that you're lazy, but it might be that you'll be starting something that you wish you hadn't.

Most of us see only what we want to see in life. Unconsciously, we edit and filter information and observations that are uncomfortable to accept. Once you've digested the big picture, you might conclude that the rift between you and your boss is irreparable. Changing yourself may only be a short-term fix. The underlying problems may be complex and not worth repairing. If you have a tyrannical, insecure boss who can't tolerate being criticized, stifling yourself in meetings may crimp your style and feelings of independence, especially if one of the things you enjoy most about your job is expressing your ideas and opinions.

That's the worst-case scenario. By the same token, you may learn that the situation is not half as bad as you thought it was. The problem may be little things such as becoming more organized, spending extra time on paperwork and book-keeping chores, or paying homage to your boss's harmless idiosyncrasies. These are adjustments that don't require overhauling your personality.

THE ENVELOPE, PLEASE

In the final analysis, it's your call. Whatever you decide to do, make sure you've examined all the facts. Face painful issues and deal with them. If you don't, they'll come back to haunt you. Initially, the truth may hurt, but in the end, it can be liberating. As hard as it is, opt for the high road. That's where you'll find the real action.

"OKAY, SO I'LL MANAGE MY BOSS"

Solution Six: Meet your boss's needs by understanding his or her motivations, habits, and work styles.

The $50 term describing the process of managing your boss is "upward management." Downward management is what bosses do to their subordinates. But no one says you, the lowly employee, can't be proactive and manage the relationship upward and achieve remarkable results, notably a better environment yielding excellent work.

Since the 1980s, battalions of management consultants have become rich by selling the concept of "managing your boss." Prestigious organizations like the American Management Association regularly stage conferences and seminars, not to mention peddling books, brochures, and audiocassettes on the subject. Process all the information on the subject and you'll discover the nucleus of upward management which, according to Joe Weintraub, a professor of management at Babson College in Wellesley, Massachusetts, simply involves "understanding your boss's world." Weintraub has lectured and written extensively on the boss-employee relationship. Once you understand your boss's world, you'll be better able to manage the conflicting relationship you have with this person.

The conflict, as you probably guessed, is more of a problem for you than it is for your boss. Your problems with your boss keep you up nights while he or she is probably sleeping like a baby. You're the one who's bent out of shape over the relationship. Despite whatever brilliant rationalizations you can conjure, you are the victim. Your boss may be trying to figure out what to do with you, but you're not the center of his or her universe. Wouldn't she be surprised to discover that most of your waking hours are consumed by your relationship? You can assume that your boss is not that concerned about making the relationship better. If you handed in your resignation today, your boss wouldn't be shattered. She'd gripe about the tedium and headache of interviewing and choosing your replacement, but I guarantee her appetite wouldn't be affected.

If you intend to manage the relationship, the burden is on you. It's not about trying to change your boss by confrontation. Instead, it's about finding out what has to be done to improve the relationship. "Many people have a hard time accepting this," says Weintraub. "Understand the ground rules and accept the fact that you're not playing on a level playing field."

But you can crawl into your boss's head to better understand his or her world. Here I'm going to show you how.

ASSESS THE SITUATION

What Does Understanding Your Boss's World Mean?

"I understand my boss," you rail. "All she cares about is making us kill ourselves so the department makes its sales quota and she comes off looking like a saint. She doesn't give a damn about us." This is an all-too-common reaction spoken like a true narcissist. I hate to shatter icons, but you're a cog in the wheel, a piece of machinery in the human assembly line—nothing more. But if you perform poorly, you'll stand out from the crowd with the spotlight on you. Now you're a problem that has to be addressed. Step away from the situation and you'll see that this picture is totally absurd. The reality is that you are only a small detail in your boss's life. If you intend to manage the relationship, you're going to have to start the process by thinking objectively. That's the crucial first step in the assessment process. But it's easier said than done. Seeing your boss's world is going to take hard work. Most bosses are terrible communicators who seldom telegraph their feelings. They keep to themselves and truly believe that they ought to maintain a discreet distance from their employees. It is only the newer highly educated generation of bosses who have been primed by industrial psychologists and have imbibed the theories of Peter Drucker and Tom Peters about bridging the boss-worker communication gap.

Traditional bosses, on the other hand, compare their roles to that of the captain of a ship. They feel they must be aloof, distant, and yes, superior to their subordinates. Accompanying that lofty role is loneliness and isolation. Like the ship's captain, they can't socialize or, heaven forbid, bare their soul to their staff. Traditional bosses believe they shouldn't get too close to someone who they may have to fire some day. In other words, they'll be better able to do their jobs if they keep their emotions in check. It sounds overly dramatic, yet there is a compelling element of truth to this kind of thinking.

Put it all together and it's easy to understand why we know so little about our bosses. Amid all the secrecy and aloofness, there lies the telling question: What makes my boss tick? Answer that $64,000 question and you've grasped the concept of upward management.

BAD SITUATIONS DON'T MEND THEMSELVES—THEY ONLY GET WORSE!

Now you have a better handle on the obstacle before you. If you agree to accept this mission, you must cross this uncharted ocean. Once you understand your boss's role, you'll be able to manage the relationship. But it's not going to happen overnight. It will take time, patience, and intensive information gathering. Despite all that has been written on the subject, most people never get past the buzzwords to understand that there is real value in managing your boss. Sadly, most of us think a bad situation will mysteriously mend itself. The thinking goes something like, "Once Norma sees how capable I am, she'll get off my back and appreciate my talents." Only in your dreams will that happen.

Somehow, we make ourselves believe we've been wronged by a cruel system. We want to believe that our demented bosses will see the light of day and say, "Lucretia, I want to apologize for my behavior over the last 6 years. The incredible work you did on the last project finally opened my eyes. It demonstrated hard work, insight, commitment, and brilliant thinking. I never realized you had such an extraordinary mind. I don't know what I've been thinking all these years. It may be late in coming, but I have to say I feel very lucky to have you on board."

If you think your boss is going to call you into his office, close the door, and mouth some variation of the above, you probably also think you're going to win the lottery. That's how remote the chances are.

Unless fate or divine intervention mysteriously alters your course for the better, bad situations only get worse. Now that I've splashed you in the face with a dose of sobering reality, let's get real and find out all we can about our boss. Here's how you do it.

THE SECRETS OF INFORMATION GATHERING

Have you given thought to how you're going to gather information about your boss? Believe it or not, the information-gathering process is actually fun. Most of your information will come simply from observing this person by stepping back and emotionally disengaging yourself from the situation. Rather than feeling persecuted and obsessing about how your boss is going to torture you next, simply hang back, listen, and observe.

By shifting your attitude, you're changing your role.

Instead of casting yourself as a lead player in this tragedy of wills, take yourself out of the drama and become an impartial critic in the audience. It's a nonthreatening role without an agenda. You'll be pleasantly shocked at what you learn. Interaction with your boss will cease to be painful. The prospect of attending meetings will no longer trigger a cold sweat. In time, you'll even look forward to them. You've also become a student. Your subject? Your boss.

Beyond observing, don't hesitate to ask questions. But be careful who you question. You don't want to seem like a snoop or a whistle-blower. *Warning:* Only approach people you trust. Even then, don't feel compelled to explain what you're doing. The less said the better. The safest response is, "I'm just trying to get a handle on Jim so I can relate to him better."

That's not a lie either. You'll accomplish little by telling anyone that your goal is to manage your boss. No matter how much you explain, people will think you've gone off the deep end. "You're what? I had no idea Jim has gotten to you this bad." Then they'll walk away convinced you've suffered a nervous breakdown.

The best people to approach are colleagues and lower-level supervisors who work with your boss. An incredible information source—if he or she talks to you and can be trusted—is your boss's secretary or assistant. *Warning:* Be careful. Approach with caution. Many secretaries who've worked closely with their bosses for several years are loyal to a fault. I've known secretaries who'd kill for their boss. Some are closer to them than they are to their spouses.

It comes down to personal chemistry. If you feel you can ask questions in an inoffensive nonthreatening way, by all means try. But if you have the slightest doubt, hesitate from proceeding. You could be hammering the nails into your own coffin. Even though your motives are noble and constructive, if this person smells skulduggery of any kind, your boss will learn of it. It's only a question of time before you're filing for unemployment insurance.

Marvelous—and safe—information sources, if you can find

them, are former employees. Since they're out of the fray, they're likely to provide startling revelations.

In the process of observing, get answers to the following questions.

WHAT DOES MY BOSS ACTUALLY DO? HOW DOES HE OR SHE DO IT?

These only seem like obvious or insulting questions. I asked several people if they could explain their bosses' jobs. All they could provide were threadbare job descriptions. An electrical engineer employed by a Fortune 500 computer hard drive manufacturer who's been grappling with his boss for 5 years said: "My boss heads a microprocessor design unit made up of five computer engineers and five electrical engineers. He sets the workloads and project scope and makes sure the work gets done."

It sounds impressive, but it doesn't say a heck of a lot. So I asked some obvious questions: How does he spend his day? What are his personal responsibilities? How does he supervise? Does he walk around and make sure everyone's working? Does he set daily quotas? How does he evaluate work? How does he handle problems or delays? Whom does he report to? The engineer was shocked that he could barely provide answers to these questions.

It was pretty much the same story with a junior buyer of children's outerwear employed by a major department store chain. When asked to describe her boss's job, she said: "She supervises all the buying of all children's outerwear, ages 3 through 12. She monitors trends, visits manufacturers, sets budgets, and helps set retail prices." Her answer triggered other questions: What does "monitoring trends" mean? Does she sit in her office reading fashion magazines? How much time is spent traveling or visiting manufacturers? Many buyers spend as much as 50 percent of their time traveling. When she's away, how does she supervise the work? When she's in the office, how does she supervise subordinates? Whom does she report to and how does she fit into the chain of command?

Other people interviewed also revealed a similar lack of knowledge about their bosses' jobs. The obvious conclusion is that most of us are so immersed in our jobs and problems that we seldom step back and find out what our bosses do and, on a broader scale, learn how their work fits into the corporate machinery. Needless to say, plenty of lazy, unproductive, and incompetent bosses exist who don't do a heck of a lot in the course of an average working day. Most, however, rank above average on the productivity scale.

More important is how bosses do their jobs. How does your boss get things done? Is he invisible or omnipresent? Some bosses have a unique habit of being everywhere and nowhere. You don't see them much, yet their powerful personalities are felt everywhere. Ideal bosses seem to be the persons who are around when you need them yet leave workers alone to do their own thing. But some bosses never leave you alone and are always stalking the halls looking over workers' shoulders. They manage to have their hands in every pot, but add little to the taste.

An industrial designer employed by a large jewelry manufacturer had strong feelings about this type of boss. He said:

> It's one thing if Jeanne knew what she was talking about. But more often than not, she's dead wrong. The upsetting part is that we have to bow to her commands. On one occasion, she had me redo a design because she thought it had flaws. It added 2 days to the project because we had to build a prototype product. Most of the designers have found a way to deal with Jeanne. If she suggests changes, we agree to them and then follow our own instincts, which are usually right.

But just as dangerous are the bosses who are never around when you need them. It usually takes a crisis to bring them out of their office to solve problems.

WHAT ARE YOUR BOSS'S HABITS, WORK STYLES, GOALS, OBJECTIVES, AND VALUES?

Believe it or not, your boss's primary goal is not to make your life miserable. You can't be that much of a narcissist. Like yourself, your boss wants things out of life. It's to your advantage to find out what they are.

Let's start with your boss's work habits and work styles. What time does he arrive every morning? Is he habitually late or early? Most of the aggressive bosses I've endured were compulsive about getting to work early. And they all did it for different reasons. What about yours? Many diligent bosses actually start work between 7 and 7:30 a.m. so they can get a head start on the day. In the early morning, without phones ringing and workers requiring their attention, they can get some serious work done, plan a meeting, sketch a proposal, prepare a complex budget, or converse with regional offices.

But I've also heard some incredible stories about goof-off bosses who get in early so their superiors and subordinates think they're diligent. Many have been caught doing a crossword puzzle or reading a novel. A few had the chutzpa to work on outside consulting assignments on company time. But the best story of all was a textile worker who barged into his boss's closed office to ask him an important question and found him huddled over a Superman comic. Now there's an eyeopener. In one awkward, naked second, this dumbfounded worker confirmed his suspicions about his boss being a blithering moron.

Once your boss arrives, what are his or her work patterns? Does she get right to work or hibernate for 30 to 40 minutes to figure out the priorities of the day? Some bosses can't wait to spring into action the moment they arrive. Some are fanatical about getting meetings over with early in the morning so the rest of the day can be spent on serious work.

A 23-year-old industrial designer for a large Minneapolis architectural firm says his boss purposely scheduled meetings at 8:30 a.m. on Mondays, the hardest day of the week to get in early, so he could separate the superstars from the slackers. Nothing slipped by him either. He knew who came in early, who charged in at the stroke of 8:30 a.m., and who habitually arrived late. What most of his workers didn't know was that he had practically a photographic eye. He saw everything and made a mental—and often a written—note of it.

How observant is your boss? This factors into his or her work style. As incredible as it seems, some bosses are oblivious to everything around them. They just assume that the work will get done and everyone is doing what they're supposed to do. Others eye their troops as if they were studying microscopic particles under an electron microscope. The message is never underestimate your boss's powers of observation.

What about your boss's goals and objectives? Many bosses with obsessive-compulsive work habits are perfectionists. Mediocrity is the enemy, and they won't tolerate slipshod work habits, laziness, or the reluctance to perform at any level but your best.

Other bosses are more concerned with simply getting the work done and meeting their quota or deadline so their boss doesn't get on their backs. They are content with just satisfactory quality. The job itself is not nearly as important as keeping their boss in check and warding off pending disasters.

How your boss feels about his work and the care and attention he gives it directly tie into his values. Bosses with strong work values are consumed with building careers. Depending on their personalities, they could be either monsters or saints. From talking to hundreds of workers, I've discovered that there doesn't seem to be any middle ground. In the process of doing an extraordinary job, they're either out for themselves or view their workers as partners in achieving exceptional results. Needless to say, the latter boss is everyone's ideal. She's the humanitarian boss everyone dreams about having. Her instincts are healthy, she's tuned into the people around her and cares about achieving harmony in the ranks. The former boss, however, can be a walking horror story if you don't perform according to his or her standards.

The primary concern is producing an exceptional product or delivering an extraordinary service. If you fail in that pursuit, you've got a problem. The megalomaniac boss who's out for himself doesn't want to hear excuses, no matter how plausible they are. He just doesn't care.

HOW DOES YOUR BOSS HANDLE PRESSURE?

Pressure affects people differently. For some, it's actually a catalyst yielding exceptional performance. I have had a couple of bosses who were nicer human beings when they were up to their eyeballs in deadlines. The more stress they had, the easier it was to work with them. Constant pressure kept them going at fever pitch. In the absence of pressure, they felt insecure, threatened, and often agitated. On the flip side, pressure can also create emotional havoc in the form of nightmares, ulcers, back pain, and a host of other physical ills.

If you're lucky, your boss has a healthy pressure tolerance. That means pressure acts as a motivator or rallying point. However, for many bosses, pressure triggers internal and external pandemonium. Watch out! Bosses may then start looking for scapegoats on which they can unleash their seething tension.

WHAT IS YOUR BOSS'S MANAGEMENT STYLE?

Typically, most bosses fall into one of two management-style camps. The first is the hands-on, all-involved boss; the other encourages independent thinking and work habits. One is no better than the other. The practitioners of either management style can be heaven or hell. Bosses who practice the former can be an encouraging asset and boost to workers under them, especially new ones, if they keep a respectful distance and don't make compulsive pests of themselves. But if they're constantly looking over your shoulder and telling you what to do, even if you're doing your job better than they could have done it, you have a problem on your hands. Not only are they annoying, but they can also be destructive.

It can go either way with the latter boss as well. A boss who encourages you to do your own thing can be a blessing if he or she gives you enough instructions and information beforehand. But if he or she is a noncommunicator who makes you go it alone no matter how difficult the assignment, you'll be anxious all the time because you're always fearfully groping in the dark. Often, you'll waste precious hours, even days, stumbling along by yourself, hoping you're doing your work properly. Needless to say, that makes for mighty stressful working conditions.

WHAT EXACTLY DOES YOUR BOSS NEED?

I'm sure you've thought a great deal about your own professional needs. Depending on order of importance, they probably include stimulating and challenging projects, amicable peers, good pay and benefits, pleasant working conditions, and advancement potential, to name a few. Those are the broad-based needs. On a personal level, you also need feedback and interaction from your peers and boss. They fall under the all-inclusive heading of communication. For many, the amount of feedback we get from our bosses often defines how we do our jobs.

But what about your boss? What are his or her career needs, both on a broad and personal level? Of course, you never thought about them. You probably figured that they were no concern of yours. But in the big picture, they are important issues, although they have nothing to do with the quality of the relationship you have with your boss. Your boss's needs amount to critical information that can help you build a strong and resilient working relationship.

Answers to the following questions can pry open doors to a better understanding of your boss:

- Is your boss the prototypical big fish in a little pond or is he or she content to be a minor player in a high-visibility company?
- What does your boss look for from underlings? Yes-people, praise/stroking, backing, or honest appraisal?
- What kinds of trappings does your boss need? Spartan cubicle or lavish office with all the amenities?

I got a variety of interesting answers to these questions. The big-fish-in-a-little-pond-type bosses seemed to be the most tyrannical. The reason is they feel most secure in small, nonthreatening organizations where they stand out and seem bigger and more effective than they actually are. They tend to be insecure, frustrated people with low self-esteem. A technician employed by a small software company had this to say:

> When I did some checking around, I learned that my boss was fired from a Fortune 500 software company. He couldn't cut it because it was too competitive. He was a low-level supervisor with five people under him, and he could barely handle all the pressure from above. Here, he has 20 people under him, and he stalks the hall like a veritable giant. He thinks he's impervious to criticism, a giant among bosses, above and beyond reproach. But anyone who's worked with him for a few years knows he's afraid of his own shadow. When his boss calls him into his office, he's an emotional basket case thinking he's screwed up or about to be fired. Knowing this, we give him exactly what he wants. We treat him like a king and make him think he's special. It's pathetic, but that's what it takes to keep him off our backs.

In describing the trappings his boss needed, a paralegal employed in a large Minneapolis law firm said:

> My boss had to be surrounded by luxury. She enjoyed setting herself apart from her workers who were confined to tiny offices. Her office was her power symbol, pointing up her wealth, ranking, and

omnipotence. By displaying expensive paintings and furniture, she was conveying a strong message that said, "I have big clients; I make a lot more money than you do. Hence, I'm untouchable and better than you—so don't screw around with me." But she also had her Achilles heel—a CEO, board of directors, and stockholders who could unseat her if they discovered she wasn't performing properly. It wasn't likely to happen, yet when paranoia got the better of her, she acted like an emotional pauper. She, too, was hungry for approval and stroking from her underlings who gladly complied.

Uncovering what bosses need from their underlings can also be an eyeopener. I learned about bosses who fell into two camps. In one camp were bosses who were terrified of making independent decisions and needed constant stroking and reassurance. In the other camp were independent bosses who were sure of themselves. They needed no feedback or reassurance from their workers. They made decisions easily and quickly. And they expected to have their orders carried out immediately with few questions asked. They didn't feel they had to overcommunicate. In fact, the less talk the better. Many saw themselves as action people who preferred to maintain a distance from their troops.

WHAT ARE YOUR BOSS'S STRENGTHS AND WEAKNESSES?

Don't say your boss has no strengths. Even wretched bosses have at least one redeeming strength. Typically, it is often a bottom-line asset (supersalesperson, money-making ideas, etc.) that landed them a supervisory job. Occasionally, organizational skills were responsible for putting some bosses in the power seat.

While some people had to wrack their brains to name one strength, they had little problem citing their bosses' weaknesses, the most common being incompetence and poor management skills. Also high on the list were the inability to make decisions and poor leadership skills.

More important than pinpointing your boss's strengths and weaknesses is understanding the effect they have on you. Typically, positive bosses don't affect us negatively. We learn and are often inspired by their strengths and understand their weaknesses. Negative bosses, however, have the opposite effect. A tyrannical, overbearing boss's strengths often intimidate shy underachievers. Weak, ineffectual bosses who ride on the coattails of their underlings infuriate fast-track superperformers. And rightfully so. They work so hard to get ahead, only to find that they have an oppressive noose around their neck.

What about yourself? Look at your own situation and think about how your boss's strengths and weaknesses impact you.

WHAT HAVE YOU LEARNED?

When you put it all together, what have you learned? And now that you've got the big picture, what are you going to do with it? Now that you have a clear picture of your boss's personality and work style, can you work together or is your only recourse finding another job?

Advice: Consider shoring up your boss's weaknesses and building on his or her strengths. Learn to fill in the gaps by making yourself indispensable. If your boss is the classic macromanager who has a difficult time dealing with a project's nitty-gritty details, pick up the slack and make sure they're handled. If he's good at analytical skills yet falters when it comes to presenting a project, help him gather the materials and organize his thoughts so that the presentation is perfect. But do it in an unobtrusive way so that you're not taking any credit for his successes.

If you're boss is a classic nitpicker and perfectionist, rev yourself up to become more detail oriented. If you're boss is obsessed with knowing intricate details, give them to him without being asked. Conversely, if your boss is a cut-to-the-chase, just-give-me-the-punch-line bottom-line person, hit her only with headlines and spare the details. Or if your boss is a power-crazy megalomaniac who must be in the spotlight, orchestrate events where he can be the star or at least stand out. Make him feel like he's the leader, one step ahead of everyone else.

A critical issue in managing your boss is always knowing the landscape. Veterans of "boss management" know what kind of mood their boss will be in before they walk in the door. Like a dog sensing his master's footsteps a block away, they know what to expect as their boss pulls into the parking lot.

Fact: Managing your boss is not about changing your boss, but accepting this person the way he or she is. Make sure you understand the difference. Many of us naively think we can actually change another person's behavior. It's not impossible, but it's a tall order. Suffice it to say that it's particularly hard in a boss-employee relationship. We'll touch on this concept briefly in the next chapter when we discuss talking to our boss one-on-one.

Successfully managing your boss represents a major undertaking. Masters of the game know their bosses better than they know themselves. They're totally in tune with their rhythms. Most important, they know their hot buttons. They know when to be invisible and when to offer advice.

Don't for a minute think that managing your boss is easy. Not everyone can pull it off. Egocentric self-absorbed people, for example, find it very difficult to step out of their own skin and into someone else's. It means suspending your ambitions long enough to understand someone else's. Some see it as a waste of time, and others see it at as huge gamble, unsure of whether it will improve the relationship.

It's your call. How badly do you want to keep your job and move up the ladder? If advancement, not to mention peace of mind, is important to you, I'd give it my best shot. What do you have to lose?

THE ADVANTAGES OF MANAGING YOUR BOSS

Summing up, ponder the advantages of managing your boss:

- Demystifies the relationship and puts it on a more equal keel by removing divisive barriers.
- Allows you to see your boss as a real person, rather than as the devil or a deity.
- Enables you to experience a sense of accomplishment if you pull it off.
- Improves your attitude, work, and career prospects.
- Gives you a priceless, transferable skill that you can use throughout your career.

"LET'S HAVE A HEART-TO-HEART"

Solution Seven: A one-on-one confrontation with your boss can produce extraordinary results—if the conditions are right. But it's also a dangerous tactic that can blow up in your face if not handled properly.

O pting for the private chat can be compared to the perilous game of Russian roulette. A cable TV executive who actually pulled it off compared it to playing catch with a hand grenade with the pin removed: One bad move and you're a memory.

A LAST-DITCH EFFORT

WHEN TO USE THIS TACTIC

The reason for a one-on-one confrontation is to present your problems so you and your boss can find a way to mend wrongs and improve the quality of the working relationship. It's a simple concept, yet one that is difficult to execute.

Understand what you are getting into. There is a world of difference between managing your boss and having a one-on-one confrontation. Attempting to manage your boss is a relatively safe strategy, whereas going for the face-to-face duel can be likened to walking into the proverbial snake pit. Understand that it is an all-or-nothing strategy.

Caution: Even if you're reasonably sure things will work out, you never know when the game may turn ugly. As Mardy Grothe and Peter Wylie wrote in *Problem Bosses,* too many things can go awry. Once you've crossed the border into the enemy camp, there is no turning back. Without warning or provocation, things can turn against you, and you'll wish you had left well enough alone. Once you've walked into your boss's office, there's no backing off. You've walked into the war zone, and like it or not, you had better be good at defending yourself.

It's your intellect, your ability to read people, and your persuasive people skills that will make this a successful confrontation. But if this strategy backfires, you'll be staring at your walking papers. *Advice:* Consider this strategy and those to follow in subsequent chapters as radical last-ditch efforts. You undertake them at substantial risk because you deem your situation intolerable.

PRELIMINARY PLANNING STEPS

IS YOUR BOSS APPROACHABLE?

THINK BEFORE YOU ACT

Advice: Don't wake up one morning full of vim and vigor and decide you're going to charge into your boss's office and demand a private meeting. That's about the dumbest thing you could do. Those adrenaline surges energize you and make you feel like you're impervious to adversity. Apply the brakes. It's only a feeling. When it comes to taking this bold step, you'll need more than jet-propelled energy. Level-headed, cool, rational thinking is what's going to guide you through the situation.

The $64,000 question that you must answer before you consider this strategy is: Is your boss approachable? Needless to say, not all bosses are. If you've forgotten, reread Chapter Four. Don't be naive. You're not going to change a loose cannon or a demented despot of Machiavellian proportions.

It's safe to say that you can reason with a mildly neurotic person. But you're wasting your time if you think you can make headway with a psychotic boss. Remember one of Sigmund Freud's basic conclusions: Crazy people are not logical.

In short, success in this kind of one-on-one encounter rests on your ability to read another human being and predict a successful outcome.

SADISTIC BOSSES PREY ON HUMAN FRAILTIES

You're a masochist if you're contemplating going one-on-one with a sadistic boss who preys on human weakness. Why, just sniffing your vulnerability or frailty is enough to put him on your tail until he's captured and imprisoned you in his web. Once in these destructive clutches, you'll likely be broken, humiliated, and stripped of dignity.

Imagine working for the manipulator bosses described by Harvey Hornstein in *Brutal Bosses and Their Prey*. When you broach the subject of getting together to discuss the possibility of improving the relationship, they'll be all ears, anxious to know what's on your mind. Once they sense you're unhappy with the relationship and wish to change it, count on them expressing heartfelt relief at your willingness to come forward to discuss the matter. But as soon as you cite specific problems in the relationship, notably counterproductive management techniques and other less than favorable tactics that create tension and anxiety in the ranks, you've made your own noose. The sad part is that you don't even know you're doing it. The cagey manipulator boss will ply you with questions, such as: "How long have you been unhappy?" or "I bet others share your feelings. You'd be helping me a great deal if you told me who else feels the same way." Naively, you find yourself unable to crawl out of the trap and, unwittingly, you tell him everything he wants to know—and more.

Just as you are about to leave his office feeling as if a giant weight has been removed from your shoulders, he'll say something like, "I'm really glad you had the integrity and the guts to come forward and talk to me openly. It's employees like you that go places and help make this company a great place to build a career."

Unfortunately, you'll realize that you've been taken when it's too late. Then it's time to watch out. Now that he knows how you and others feel about him, he'll be gunning for you. Unwittingly, you signed your own death warrant. Just when you least expect it, he's going to drop some huge bombs that will embarrass or humiliate you and stall your career. If he's cruelly vindictive, as many crazy bosses are, he may even find a way to get you fired. Manipulator bosses are good at that. For some, it's practically a sport. It takes real creativity, albeit warped, to manipulate your way up the career ladder. Don't think there aren't CEOs who cleverly manipulated their way to the top slot in Fortune 500 companies. They've mastered a dangerous game few people understand.

Can My Boss Actually Hear What I'm Saying?

Once you get a reading on your boss's mental state, determine whether this person has the ability to listen to what you have to say and critically evaluate its merit. Not everyone in authority is capable of doing that. Ultimately, it means taking an objective look at yourself in terms of your effect on others. If your boss gets high marks on this count, I'd start revving up the wheels for the one-on-one encounter.

Let's lay the groundwork for the dreaded meeting.

PLANNING THE MEETING

Put Your Grievances on Paper First

Joe Weintraub, an expert on deviant bosses and a professor of management at Babson College, in Wellesley, Massachusetts, suggests planning out the one-on-one meeting. "The key to successful planning is knowing the personality of the person with whom you're going to be meeting," he says. "The approach you take with a boss from hell is very different than the one you'd take with a Felix Unger-type boss."

Weintraub advises thinking about what you want to say to your boss and then writing a memo—which you're not going to send—outlining everything you'd like to say. The process puts everything in perspective. Seeing your grievances on paper puts a realistic spin on the issue, which you're not likely to consider when merely contemplating the confrontation.

In fact, read your memo aloud so you can get an idea of the impact it will have. Ask yourself, "Would airing my grievances with my boss be a career-limiting move? Simply, what impact would it have on my future?"

"If you're looking at the encounter honestly and objectively, you see both risks and rewards," says Weintraub. The risks ought to be obvious. If you blurt out the wrong words, you look like a fool. If you inadvertently insult your boss, you'll be collecting unemployment insurance within weeks. The rewards are enlightenment and the exchange of critical information which lead to a healthier and more productive relationship between you and your boss.

Advice: Make sure your grievances are work-related and can be substantiated. Don't assume that your boss is conscious of wrongdoing. Be prepared to cite specific projects and actual events where your boss treated you cruelly or unfairly. Stay clear of personal issues that have no bearing on your job. Don't try to change your boss's habits. That's not why you're there. Instead, stick to relationship issues that negatively affect the way you and your boss work together.

Before I outline tips and procedures for conducting a smooth encounter, here is what to avoid.

SAMPLE MEETING

ENCOUNTER GONE WRONG

The following worker, Sam, figured he'd try the one-on-one encounter. With little preparation, he impulsively decided to go for it. Here's what happened when he walked into his boss's office to put his cards on the table.

SAM: Sally, if you don't mind, I'd like to have a few words with you. I hope this is a good time.

SALLY: Well, actually, it's not the best time because I'm kind of rushed. I have an important luncheon meeting with a prospective client in about 30 minutes and I am preparing my thoughts. So let's make it fast. It seems like you have something to get off your chest.

SAM: You're right, Sally. I've got a big problem. To be perfectly honest, the problem is *you*. I don't know whether you are aware of it, Sally, but you're impossible to work with. If you think I'm speaking out of turn, just ask anyone else in the department. Everyone will agree with me. The only difference between me and the others is that I had the guts to come in and speak my mind. Am I making sense?

SALLY: You're making perfectly good sense, Sam. Tell me more.

SAM: I hope you don't mind me being totally honest.

SALLY: Not at all. You're off to a good start. So why don't you put all your cards on the table, Sam?

SAM: You're probably not aware of it, but the biggest issue I have with you is your overbearing, combative management style. Sadly, there is only one way of doing things around here—it's your way. Maybe you don't realize it, but there are plenty of talented people in this company. You wouldn't know that because you don't give people a chance to express their opinions. There are engineers and technical people who have been here for 15 years. Over that kind of time period, you learn a lot. I'm not saying you don't know your stuff, but you've only been here for 4 years. I doubt if you know how capable these people are.

Take last week's meeting. I got up to talk about a proposed ventilation system for the new office building project. Before I could explain the premise of my idea, you cut me off and said it wouldn't work. When Ted chimed in to support what I was saying, you shut him up, too. That's no way to work with people. I'm not saying you're not a good engineer. I know you went to MIT and graduated at the top of your class, but there are people here who came from less well-known schools who are just as capable.

I'm telling you all this so you can think about stepping back and giving other people a chance. You're not the only person who is building a career. We're all trying to get ahead. I know you're in a rush. But maybe we can get together next

week and talk some more about improving our working relationship. Maybe I'll bring some of the other people, too. A little discussion is all it takes to make things better. How does
that sound?

SALLY: This conversation was a real eyeopener for me. I want to
thank you for telling me how things really are. Yes, indeed.
You can count on us talking about this in greater detail.

THE PSYCHOLOGY OF CONFRONTATION

What do you think of the way Sam handled his one-on-one
chat with his boss? Do you think he made his point and was
successful? Do you think his boss was appreciative? Will anything positive come of it?

Unfortunately, Sam blew it. It will be a miracle if he keeps
his job. In this brief conversation, he managed to break all the
cardinal rules of productive confrontation. To appreciate the
depth of his mistakes, let's first ponder some facts of human
confrontation. Bob Abramms, a psychologist who heads the
management consulting firm ODT, Inc., in Amherst,
Massachusetts, says, "A basic principle of human behavior is
people rarely change under duress." It can be likened to walking up to someone and taking a swing at them. Naturally, the
other person is going to defend himself by hitting back. In the
case of a verbal assault, Abramms says, "The human psyche
kicks in with denial, rejection, closure, and a battery of
defense mechanisms—psychological dynamics which make it
impossible to change under assault."

I didn't include Sally's rebuttal in the foregoing fictional
conversation, but you can sense her displeasure with Sam's
candid comments. You're right in assuming that she will retaliate using all the power she can muster. Sam will wish he never
crossed her threshold to speak his mind.

Advice: The worst thing you can do in a one-on-one confrontation is put your boss on the defensive. The most productive strategy is to begin the conversation by putting the onus
on yourself, not your boss.

Sam never considered that basic tenet of human psychology. Look at his confrontational opening remarks: "I've got a big problem. To be perfectly honest, the problem is *you.*" In 10 seconds, he managed to alienate his boss. After that, it only gets worse. "I don't know whether you are aware of it, Sally, but you're impossible to work with. If you think I'm speaking out of turn, ask anyone else in the department."

Not only does he hit his boss on the head with a verbal sledgehammer, but he also has the audacity to say that everyone else feels the same way he does. He's implying there is strength in numbers and that Sally doesn't stand a chance. He thinks he can actually get away with ganging up on his boss.

The situation continues to deteriorate. Sam goes on to tell his boss exactly what he thinks of her, calling her "overbearing" and "combative." He doesn't stop there. He pulls out all the stops by telling her that she's a control freak who must have her way, that other engineers on staff are just as competent, and that she ought to back off and let them have their say. She might learn something.

Sam's insensitive tirade only sounds exaggerated. As incredible as it may seem, thoughtless bursts of honesty like this happen every day.

WHOEVER SAID HONESTY IS THE BEST POLICY?

When it comes to the art of human interaction, forget all the homespun homilies you were taught as a kid. This is one instance where honesty is not the best policy. Heed Weintraub's advice, "If you practice total honesty in any organization, the next seminar you'll be going to is the resume-writing workshop."

Only in the movies do bosses say lines like, "Hey, John, thanks for sharing your thoughts about your opinion of me." According to Weintraub, "Bosses are not that open-minded and understanding." "They're more likely to say, 'Good luck on your next job and don't let the door hit you on your way out.'"

Remember: While freedom of speech is a basic human right granted by the U.S. Constitution, it doesn't exist in the workplace. If you don't believe me, speak to the millions of people who work for crazy bosses. Adds Weintraub, "You're a fool if you're totally honest and say what you think."

However, there is one instance when you can tell your boss exactly what you think of him or her: when you have another job.

DOING THE ONE-ON-ONE CONFRONTATION TWO-STEP: IT'S SIMPLE IN CONCEPT BUT DIFFICULT TO MASTER

Now that we've outlined some of the snafus of confronting your boss, here are some helpful guidelines so you don't trip yourself.

- Keep your emotional level low. Don't attempt a confrontation when feeling stressed. Naturally, you're going to be nervous, but avoid coming across as jittery, tense, or highstrung.

- Don't come on too strong. Pace yourself by starting off slowly. Rather than jumping right into the business at hand, establish a comfortable rapport by making small talk.

- Present problems diplomatically and carefully, all the while enlisting your boss's help. If you want your boss to change, put yourself in his or her hands. Abramms advises saying something like, "The way we are working together isn't meshing. What can I do to change?"

- Be descriptive in defining the problem you are having.

SAMPLE CONFRONTATION

Weintraub offers this fictional exchange between a worker and his boss, whom we'll call Sidney:

> Sidney, I'd like to tell you about a problem I'm having. I need your help. Yesterday, you asked me to come to the staff meeting with two ideas for improving the engineering project. When I started speaking, you cut me off three times. I was just wondering what was going on. I was trying to explain a new marketing strategy I developed. It made me feel like I wasn't very important. I need your help in trying to understand what happened. What did I do that was wrong?

STEP BACK AND HEAR
WHAT YOUR BOSS HAS TO SAY

Once you diplomatically state the problem, allow your boss to present his side of the story. This is a critical juncture, says Weintraub: "Once you've tersely outlined the problem, toss the ball back in his corner and see what he has to say."

More likely than not, your boss might express total ignorance over his behavior. Since you were so forthright and diplomatic, he may offer no defense and come back with, "I had no idea I did that. I'm sorry you felt that way. It wasn't my intention." Or he may make an excuse. "I've been a little edgy as of late. The top brass is leaning on me to increase our sales quotas and I guess I've been dumping on everyone around me." After your boss expresses an initial reaction, he might say, "What do you suggest I do about it?"

That's the opening you've been waiting for. You might say, "Well, Sidney, if you were to ream us individually, I'd like permission to call you on it. I'd like to say, 'Hey, Sidney, you did it again.' But as you can gather from the way I'm approaching this delicate subject, I feel uncomfortable about bringing this up."

Caution: Weintraub urges extreme caution in attempting

to call your boss on his bad behavior. Even congenial bosses who don't have a clue about what's happening around them may get offended at presumptuous behavior from their employees. "This is dangerous territory," warns Weintraub, "so don't push your luck."

Remember: You're not on equal footing with your boss. You can't say, "If this happens again, Sidney, it's your job." It sounds wonderful, but the reality is you can't fire your boss. But you can describe how his actions impact you and your performance.

Advice: The goal is to get your boss to think about his or her bad behavior. Only discuss your actions in terms of yourself. Do not discuss how they affect other people. Only champion your own cause. State your case diplomatically and tactfully, advises Weintraub: "Use phrases like 'Here is what I am experiencing.' Or 'Here is how I felt when that was happening.' Then be silent and let the boss respond. Often, he or she is unaware of these actions."

Weintraub goes on to say that most bosses aren't jerks intentionally. "If you call them on something," he adds, "they may back off and say, 'I really didn't mean to do that.'"

The moral of the story is that there is no accounting for human behavior. Just when you think you have someone figured out, your boss pulls a surprise, proving that things often aren't what they seem to be.

Weintraub and other experts advise testing the waters cautiously. If you want your boss to change, place the burden on yourself. Then sit back and watch the landscape change.

Says management consultant Abramms: "People are often inspired by other people who model the ability to change. If the onus is on the employee, it may subliminally trigger a shift in the personality dynamics of the relationship. Rather than playing an emotional tug-of-war with your boss, put yourself in his hands. You'll be pleasantly surprised by the results."

Remember, only discuss your feelings. Your boss can't refute or disagree with them. They're entirely yours, and no one can dispute them. Your feelings are ultimately your strongest tool for making headway. If you said, "I really feel meaningless in terms of the work we are doing," your boss can't say, "No, you don't feel that way." By expressing your feelings, you're disarming your boss, says Weintraub. "It puts the other person in the mode of having to do some work and reflection."

If you hit pay dirt, the boss might say, "Give me an example." Suddenly, the sky opens and you can cite real examples, which your boss, on reflection, won't be able to dispute. Be prepared and come to the meeting with comments and suggestions.

DON'T EXPECT YOUR BOSS
TO TAKE THE FIRST STEP

YOU MUST INITIATE THE CHANGE PROCESS

Abramms and other experts suggest that one-on-one confrontations stand their best chance of succeeding if you prove you are willing to do everything possible to make the relationship work. "Don't expect your boss to take the first step," says Abramms. By initiating the first step, you're reconfirming the power boundaries.

What does it matter that you think it's all hogwash? Your real feelings don't count here. This is about building your career, not about being sincere.

In short, tell your boss what he or she wants to hear. "Once you model a willingness to change, you are creating the foundation for a relationship," adds Abramms.

ABSOLUTE NO-NO:
DON'T WALK IN WITH A SCRIPT

As I said earlier, confronting your boss is a dangerous tactic. Naturally, you're nervous and you want to do everything possi-

ble to make sure things go well. As anxious as you are, don't
walk in with a script. That will immediately put your boss on
the defensive. However, it is okay to bring a few bullet points
jotted down on a note pad which you can casually refer to in
the course of conversation so you hit all the high points.
Remember: Even though you've been prepared for weeks, your
performance must come across as a casual conversation, not
as a rehearsed scene.

WHEN AND WHERE TO STAGE
THE MEETING

The time and place of the meeting are critical. Privacy must
be assured. That means a comfortable place where you can
speak freely. Informal places such as restaurants, bars, or coffee shops are not a good idea for obvious reasons. You risk
running into colleagues or executives, which can only add to
your difficulties, especially if it's no secret you're having problems with your boss. It wouldn't take much for anyone to size
up the reason for the meeting.

The two best places for the meeting are a conference room
or your boss's office. No one would have second thoughts
about seeing you in either setting. While you may not have
control over the place, I prefer the former location because it's
a neutral setting. Naturally, your boss is going to feel more at
home in his own office. His office is his pulpit where he
wreaks havoc. If you remove him from that setting, you stand
a better chance of communicating. However, all you can do is
suggest the place. Your boss will pick the one he deems most
comfortable.

The time of the meeting is also critical. Use common sense
and pick a time of the week or month when the pace is slower
and more relaxed. Don't pick a deadline day or the last day of
the quarter when tension and stress are often at explosive levels. Instead, try for a neutral and calm day when it's just business as usual. Two ideal times that are not apt to draw atten-

tion to your mission are midday and after work. Early morning, before the business day officially starts, can be an unsettling time because people are arriving. Many offices tend to get busy very early.

Advice: Determine the suggested place and time prior to the meeting. Casually toss out the suggestions as if they just occurred to you. Unless your boss has strong feelings about time and place, he'll go along with your suggestions. If broached in an offhanded friendly way, there is no reason why he should object.

Remember: "Casual" and "friendly" are the operative words in getting your way. It could be as effortless as, "Joan, I'd like to grab about 20 minutes of your time? How does 5:15 p.m. in the small conference room sound?" Chances are, she'll come back with, "No problem. I'll see you then."

Or, if she doesn't like the place for the meeting, she might say, "Let's meet in my office instead." End of story. The stage is set. Your job is to show up at the appointed hour and be brilliant.

FINAL THOUGHTS AND SUGGESTIONS

Don't Expect Miracles

The best advice is "know your customer." If your gut tells you that a heart-to-heart is a dangerous tactic, avoid it at all costs. *Advice:* It's naive to think that all people have the capacity to change. Many people are incapable of doing so. Even a lobotomy wouldn't help some bosses because they don't have the emotional and intellectual wherewithal to change or maybe they're simply too stupid. In either situation, you are spitting into the proverbial wind.

Even if your boss is approachable, don't expect miracles. It's unreasonable to expect complete victory or total satisfaction. Even if your boss sees your point of view and owns up to bad behavior, don't expect a complete metamorphosis after your conversation. The best you can hope for are small positive changes that improve your situation. Whatever gains are made, consider them a victory. If nothing else, you've improved and opened up the communication lines, which amount to major accomplishments in their own right.

If you want to take a utopian stance, you'll walk away from the meeting with a greater understanding of your boss.

Now let's move on to a popular escape tactic from demonic bosses: transferring to a new department.

"SO I'LL TRANSFER TO A NEW DEPARTMENT"

Solution Eight: Transferring to a new department is a neutral strategy that can work if executed strategically.

If managing your boss and arranging a one-on-one confrontation aren't good options, consider bailing out and transferring to a new department. Bear in mind that this solution receives mixed reviews. It works best under optimal conditions, but even then, strategy and caution are recommended.

HIGH MARKS AS A TEMPORARY MEASURE

As a temporary measure, it is virtually a fail-safe technique. If you're working for an obnoxious despot who's blocking your every move, a transfer to a new department can be likened to a brief stop at a way station until you find a new job.

Jim, a computer programmer, is a good example of someone who successfully used this strategy. Jim recently left a mid-size company to join a large engineering company as a senior programmer. But 8 months prior to leaving his job, he transferred to a new department to get away from an unreasonable boss. But there was a rub. As Jim tells it:

> I was in the classic I-love-my-job-but-hate-my-boss situation. And there was no way to rectify it. We were the same age, yet he lacked experience. It sounds boastful, but I was a much better programmer, and he knew it. This was the cause of all our problems. His

promotion to supervisor exemplified corporate politics at its worst. An executive vice president owed a powerful vendor a favor and hired his brother—my boss—who supposedly came highly recommended. But that didn't do me much good. As soon as he looked at my work and checked out my credentials, he knew he was outmatched. In a low-key way, he did everything possible to undermine my work and make me look bad in front of management.

When I turned in a project for review, he took weeks to get back to me with comments, which were usually negative. But the incident that told me my situation was hopeless was when he had me rework a project I had been working on for 2 months, including weekends. I poured my heart and soul into developing an intricate software application for an important client. What's more, I knew it worked because I had a programmer friend critique and test it. I find it a great way to get an objective opinion about my work from someone I trust. When my boss gave the project a thumbs down, I faced up to the fact that my situation was unsalvageable. If I didn't do something soon, it would only get worse. That's when I decided to look for a new job. Thankfully, the market for programmers was incredible. There were plenty of jobs. The trick was finding the right one.

Through a friend, Jim found what he thought was the perfect job. The only hitch was it wouldn't be vacant for 8 months, which meant Jim had to endure more torture. As a temporary measure, he thought he'd transfer to a new department. Thanks to a reorganization in another department, an opening occurred and Jim jumped on it. His new supervisor knew why he was transferring and welcomed him with open arms.

TALENT WINS OUT

VALUED WORKERS STAND THE BEST CHANCE OF MAKING A SMOOTH TRANSFER

Jim was lucky. Not only did he find a better job, but he was able to find an ally who okayed the transfer. When he left the firm, his new supervisor understood and supported the move.

Even if he didn't have someone in his corner, the temporary move would have been easy to pull off because he had great credentials. And even if he blundered and explained the reasons for his transfer, another department head would have scooped him up. In the programming community, creativity is highly valued.

Jim's story proves that talent wins out. The industry you're in or the nature of your work doesn't matter. If you're a rising star, you usually have a great deal of mobility.

BIG COMPANIES OFFER THE BEST TRANSFER OPPORTUNITIES

The bigger the company, the easier it is to transfer to a new department, provided you have the right qualifications. In many large companies, a transfer amounts to a long bureaucratic procedure that can often take months to execute. There's paperwork, procedures, and endless delays. That's the bad news. The good news is that large companies are more likely to give you the opportunity to start over.

If you've got a sense of adventure, a transfer can also be a very exciting and prudent career move. Sprawling conglomerates and international companies, for instance, regularly post positions in different parts of the country, even the world. Depending on how mobile and flexible you are, you may be able to pull off a transfer to another part of the country.

Susan, a bilingual administrative assistant employed by a Fortune 500 company, recently transferred from the New York corporate headquarters to a San Francisco regional office. It amounted to a major lifestyle move, which was endorsed by her husband, a high school history teacher. Says Susan, "I was lucky because my husband also wanted to move to California. He decided to give up his job and find another in San Francisco. After teaching in one school for 8 years, it amounted to a major change. If he wanted to keep his job and stay in New York, I would have understood and not requested the transfer.

But we both wanted to see what it was like living and working in a different part of the country."

There are other advantages to transferring to another division or office. Many people who endorse the transfer option say it's like working for a new company. Although your paychecks are still being cut by the parent company, you may be pleasantly surprised to encounter new work styles.

The corporate culture of a regional office is often very different from that of the home office. Trudy works for a large national Boston-based apparel company. She recently transferred to a regional office 40 miles away to free herself from a tyrannical boss who was making her life miserable. Trudy describes the change: "It felt like I was taking a new job. The central office is tense, fast-paced, and very competitive, whereas the atmosphere at the regional office is more casual and laid back. Most of the people don't seem as obsessed and frantic about building careers. Maybe it has to do with the fact that the regional office is located in a suburban/rural community and the main office is in a big city."

But Trudy also observes that the downside to working in a regional office was a lower likelihood of strategic promotions. "There are promotional opportunities no matter where you work in the company," she goes on, "but the best ones are in the home office because it is where major decisions are made. This is where senior management sets policy and doles out promotions. It's the only place to be if you're intent on moving up the ladder."

Tyrone discovered a similar situation when he transferred to a regional office of a major shoe manufacturer. He had to get away from a power-obsessed paranoid boss who felt Tyrone was after his job. Unfortunately, Tyrone wound up hurting his career by taking a sales job at a regional office. Over his decade-long stay with the company, he had worked hard to become one of the company's top producers. For 3 straight years, he won vacations all over the globe for turning in outstanding performances. Management had its eye on him, and corporate scuttlebutt had it that one day he'd be promoted to an executive slot. It was well known that the most direct route to the executive suite was via sales. But once Tyrone moved to a regional office, he slipped out of management's sightlines and hampered his chances of promotion.

It's possible to be promoted to a power job in a regional office or even to be transferred back to the home office for a better position; nonetheless, strategic promotional opportunities are a lot more difficult to negotiate.

GETTING LOST IN THE CROWD

Even if you don't pack your things and transfer to another company office, you can still get a new start by transferring to a new department within the same building. Corporate offices of many large companies amount to towering skyscrapers with 30 to 50 floors. Workers often don't know who is working on the floor beneath or above them. The advantage of transferring within a large company is that it's easy to get lost in the crowd and start over.

WHEN TRANSFERRING
CAN BE DANGEROUS

Attempting a transfer in a start-up, small, or family-run company could be a serious mistake. Generally, the smaller the company, the more dangerous the move.

Small companies are often incestuous communities and hotbeds of gossip. They can be likened to small towns where privacy is a myth. Even if you attempt to execute a transfer tactfully, count on everyone knowing about it. Most small organizations breed powerful and virulent grapevines where gossip quickly finds its way from the loading dock to the corporate suite. Even if you've covered your tracks by burying the true reason for a transfer, assume veteran staffers will discover your real motives. And even if they're wrong, within hours of your move, everyone will know you transferred to get clear of a despotic boss.

Also expect to be treated as if you are a failure or malcontent. Even though you're trying to get away from a raving lunatic, many staffers will label you a quitter who couldn't take the heat. It can be even worse in small family-run organizations where family members control every rung of the organizational ladder.

As is the case in many large companies, family-run companies can be beset with political problems triggered by jealousy and the quest for power and money. For example, low-ranking family members have a tough time moving up, yet it's doubly hard, often impossible, for outsiders to wield power.

A lateral move, even under the most innocuous conditions, will be looked upon with a certain degree of skepticism. Before knowing the details, the assumption may be that there is a malcontent in our ranks.

Caution: You could be putting your career on the line by requesting a transfer in a family-managed company, especially if the demon you're fleeing is a family member. If the family member is low on the totem pole, maybe you stand a chance. But if he or she wields any power, think twice about opening your mouth. You can figure out the repercussions.

Advice: Regardless of the type of company, try to negotiate a low-profile transfer. The quieter the better.

CASE STUDIES

To best illustrate how to execute a smooth transfer, let's follow two people through the process. It won't take you long to figure out who made the right moves.

HENRY'S STORY

Henry was employed by a large engineering firm, having worked his way up from associate engineer to senior project manager. After putting in 12 years, he commanded a good deal of respect. But at this precarious point in his career, Henry was very unhappy. Without warning, a companywide reorganization resulted in his reporting to a boss 20 years his junior. They had an immediate clash of personalities. For all the obvious reasons, both men despised each other and there was no disguising their hatred. Henry's boss was an Ivy League graduate who landed his job because of political clout. His father was a high-ranking member of the board of directors who literally handed his son the supervisory job without consulting anyone.

Henry, on the other hand, was a hardworking engineer who came up through the ranks. He earned his engineering degree by attending a state college at night while working days. Henry started at the bottom; his boss started at the top. Henry was experienced and knowledgeable; his boss was a novice.

Henry knew he had a problem the moment he clapped eyes on his young boss. For 6 months, he tried to make a go of it. But not a day went by when the young man wasn't blocking him or interfering with his work. He savagely criticized Henry's work and decision-making power. Almost always, the boss was wrong.

Henry couldn't take it anymore and wanted out. He had no intention of leaving the company for which he had worked hard to build a career. Instead, he decided to transfer to a new department. He figured anything was better than working for an incompetent bungler.

But Henry was very vocal about his feelings. He was anything but discreet. There wasn't a person who didn't know about his hatred for his new boss. He complained to his buddies on the loading docks as well as to colleagues, supervisors, and secretaries.

He started the transfer process by speaking to the director of his company's human resources department, who already knew about his problem. Bad news travels fast. The director of human resources bluntly told him that it would be difficult making a clean break because everyone knew how he felt about his boss. Henry was told that a transfer would be approved, but it wouldn't be a smooth transition in light of the bad feelings between the two men. But that wasn't half the story. Henry's transfer request also became a political issue. Getting away from a bad boss is difficult enough, but this one happened to be a well-placed manager.

Despite the human resource manager's good intentions, finding a new home for Henry wasn't easy. Although Henry boasted an impressive track record, many supervisors didn't want him in their departments because he was deemed a loose cannon. Suddenly, everyone forgot about Henry's past accomplishments. Instead, he was viewed as a wild man who couldn't keep his mouth shut and make peace with a bad situation. The water-cooler scuttlebutt went something like, "So Henry can't get on with his boss. What's the big deal? How many people can?" The thinking was that he should have kept quiet and just coped with a bad situation like employees have done since the beginning of time.

It took several weeks to find a department that would welcome Henry. But even after he got what he wanted, things were never the same.

The unhappy conclusion to this story is that Henry wound up leaving the company a year after he transferred to the new department. His transfer turned out to be a bad solution.

JUDY'S STORY

Judy also had grave problems with her boss. But unlike Henry, who inherited a bad boss, Judy was saddled with Sally, an insecure and incompetent boss, the moment she joined a large cosmetics firm as a marketing coordinator 3 years ago. Her situation was a delicate one. Sally had been with the company for 15 years. She began working nights as a clerk and gradually moved up to a senior marketing slot. Nobody knows how she did it because she wasn't the brightest person at the company. What's more, her decision-making powers left something to be desired. But Sally was a hard worker and she was persistent, which landed her successive promotions. As Woody Allen observed, there is something to be said for just showing up.

For more than 2 years, Judy tried to make the best of a tough situation. As she learned more, her confidence level grew. She had many good ideas that should have been developed and tested. They could have meant increased sales for the company and promotions for Judy. The problem was that Sally blocked her. Sally knew Judy was a shining star, but she was afraid she would undermine her own position in the firm. These feelings weren't unfounded either. So she made Judy feel uncomfortable and inadequate. Sally knew that Judy was a natural marketing person. She had insight and creative instincts that Sally lacked. Judy had a knack for analyzing a situation and coming up with a great solution. Sally, on the other hand, would agonize over decisions and often wind up making bad ones. There was no way Sally could endorse, encourage, and promote Judy. In her mind, she'd be threatening her own position in the firm.

Judy knew this and decided that the only way she could find an outlet for her talents was to transfer to another department. But Judy also realized that to make a smooth transition to a new department she had to proceed cautiously and strategically. It had to be meticulously planned down to the last detail, and it would take time to execute.

Instinctively, Judy knew she had to pave the way by building support on all fronts. First, she had to find a new home within the company. Being an outgoing person with friends everywhere, she found a number of departments that would welcome her with open arms. She picked a department with products she felt would be a good fit for her background.

Then Judy began to lay the foundation for her move. She spoke to the supervisor of the new department about her desire to switch. She diplomatically left Sally out of the conversation. She explained the reason for her move was to gain experience working with new products and to learn more about the business. She made a point of saying she felt lateral moves within a company are an excellent career-building strategy. The supervisor agreed. Judy left knowing she had an ally.

She picked a supervisor who would encourage her to grow and express herself. She was right. The supervisor said she would endorse the transfer if Sally agreed to let Judy leave.

Now that she had a place to go, the most difficult part of the transfer was still ahead: getting Sally to approve the move. Judy knew that if she presented her case properly, Sally would welcome the move and be glad to get rid of her.

On a slow day, Judy knocked on Sally's door and asked to speak to her privately. She said she enjoyed working with Sally and had learned a lot from her. But at this point in her career, she wanted another product area so she could gain new insights into the business. She went on about how much she loved the business, emphasizing that she was restless and wanted to try something different. Then she told her where she wanted to move. The reasons were twofold: the products intrigued her and the department was shorthanded. She also said the supervisor of the department would endorse the transfer if Sally approved it.

Cleverly, Judy kept the discussion to business issues, avoiding any hot buttons that might jinx her chances of getting the transfer. Never once did she mention the problems in their relationship. Telling Sally that she was responsible for putting her career on hold wasn't going to work in her favor. Judy judiciously avoided any explosive issues.

The tactic worked immediately. Once Judy spelled out the facts, Sally's face lightened and she said she appreciated her honesty. She understood that she wanted to learn more and would do everything in her power to make sure the transfer went through. Of course, Judy knew Sally couldn't wait to get rid of her. She also knew that Sally secretly hoped she would take a new job. Transferring to another department turned out to be ideal.

Just as Judy got up to leave, Sally said she would miss her and that she had been a valuable asset. Judy almost choked when she heard that, but she managed to smile graciously.

Three weeks later, Judy packed her things and moved to the new department. She felt good knowing she had secured a smooth transfer, not an easy feat by any stretch of the imagination.

ANALYSIS: COOL, CALM DELIBERATION MAKES FOR A SMOOTH TRANSFER

Using the two case studies as examples, here's how to execute a smooth transfer.

Deal Only with Business Issues.   A big mistake is making your transfer a personal issue. Corporations, although they won't admit it, prefer to deal with business, not personal issues. You're there to do a job. Period. Companies pride themselves on hiring team players. Even though human resources and employee relations departments are supposed to deal with problem employees and personality disputes, they deem them a tedious annoyance that they'd rather avoid. If you have a problem with another employee or with your boss, they prefer you solve it yourself.

If you want to get away from a demon boss, find a business reason for the transfer. That's exactly what Judy did. She told her boss, along with anyone else who asked, that the reason for the transfer was to work on new products and to learn more about the business. It's hard to dispute bottom-line logic. But if you mention a personality dispute, you'll muddy the situation with nonbusiness issues.

Remember the credo of most businesses: Profits are more important than people.

Keep Your Emotions in Check.   When you're angry or feel upset about something, it's often difficult to think rationally and objectively. Unfortunately, Henry couldn't pull in the reins on his emotions, which meant he was operating at a distinct disadvantage. Fueled by his outrage, he managed to do everything wrong and put his foot in his mouth every step of the way. The results were disastrous. If you hope to pull off a successful transfer, check your emotions at the door.

Plan Your Transfer Carefully.   Judy planned and executed the transfer as if playing a game of chess. Every move was carefully thought out for its ultimate effect. Unlike Henry, she made no rash moves. All her work paid off. Not only did she get her transfer, but it turned out to be a smart career move in the process.

Don't Burn Bridges: Make Friends, Not Enemies.   The main idea is to build relationships, not destroy them. That is precisely what Judy did. Henry, however, never thought of the consequences of alienating his boss. He was doubly foolish by failing to consider his boss's position in the managerial hierarchy. If he ever considered how much power his boss wielded, he never would have attempted the transfer.

Another major faux pas was trying to execute the transfer through the company's human resources department. By doing so, he elevated his problem to a minor company crisis involving many levels. As soon as it was aired in human resources, every major department head knew about Henry's problems.

Judy, however, found a new home within the company herself, never involving the human resources department. When a transfer is negotiated correctly, the human resources department will be the last to know about it. After all, its function is to oversee the staffing process. If the initial search-and-find process is negotiated by managers, the human resources department has nothing more to do than process the paperwork.

Maybe Henry would have stood a remote chance of pulling off the transfer if he first found a department that needed him and a supervisor who appreciated his talents. Instead, he created havoc by burning bridges all around him.

Be Discreet.   Whatever you do, don't tell everyone within earshot that you're planning a transfer because you hate your boss. Be very careful who you confide in. Only confide in people you trust implicitly. The fewer people you tell, the better. If the wrong person should hear about your plans, the rumor mill will be primed, and you'll be put in the uncomfortable position of having to defend yourself.

Consider the Timing of Your Move.   Finally, timing must be considered. Plan your transfer at a time when you can command the necessary support and attention. Don't even think of attempting a transfer at busy times of the month or during deadlines. During crises or critical earnings periods, employee transfers are considered trivial matters that no manager wants to think about.

Don't Lose Sight of Your Goals.   Don't forget why you're going through the trouble of transferring to another department. It's not to vent your spleen or get even with a crazy boss, but to get on with your career in a better setting. If you keep yourself centered with those goals dead ahead, you stand a good chance of achieving them.

If you think transferring is dangerous, going above your boss's head can be akin to committing corporate suicide if done incorrectly. Let's find out how to pull it off.

"I CAN'T TAKE IT ANYMORE. I'M TALKING TO THE BIG GUY!"

Solution Nine: Think twice about going above your boss's head.
It's a last-ditch effort for the courageous.

If you think transferring to a new department is scary, going above your boss's head is the most dangerous tactic of all. Consider this true story from a few years ago when companies across the country were deep into cutting their ranks with little concern about the repercussions.

Ted was a product manager of a national beverage company whose popular products are sold in supermarkets across the nation. After 15 great years with the company, a well-publicized takeover changed everything. Until that dreaded day, Ted ran a tight unit consisting of 50 people he had brought up through the ranks. Each one was handpicked, dedicated, and hardworking. Ted was a great person to work for, and it was easy to understand why his employees worshiped him.

Until his life unexpectedly changed, Ted had it made. His competence was rewarded with free reign from a high-ranking vice president who appreciated Ted's talents.

Like most corporate managers, Ted followed the business news closely. He knew the American business machine was in the throes of change. Yet, like thousands of others who loved their jobs, he never imagined his company would be taken over by a powerful international conglomerate, causing havoc.

His utopian position in the company ended when his boss was fired and replaced by a heartless martinet intent on overhauling Ted's department. It didn't matter that the department had one of the highest productivity quotas in the company.

Ted's new boss felt compelled to change things just for the sake of change. He was intent on exerting his authority. Ted likened it to an invading army trashing the countryside and killing everything in sight in a dramatic show of power. For no reason at all, Ted's new boss fired half his department. After the last person was terminated, Ted was called in and read the riot act. His boss neither defended nor rationalized his actions. He merely laid out the game plan. He told Ted that things were going to be done differently. A new commander was in place, and he'd better shape up or he'd also get his walking papers.

What saved Ted was his impressive track record. Somehow they couldn't bring themselves to put him out to pasture. The decision wasn't made out of appreciation; it was simply good business. Ted was a valuable and consistent producer. What's more, he was a hero to the younger workers. Everyone knew Ted's story of working his way through the ranks. He did it not by playing corporate politics, but through sheer hard work. The new management deemed him potentially valuable. Why not give him an opportunity to cope with the new regime?

PLANNING TO DO BATTLE

Ted didn't think too much of the meager crumbs they were offering. He had too much pride and self-esteem to feel gratitude for being a survivor. In fact, he felt guilty because he thought he let his coworkers down by not protesting the firings. But he knew there was nothing he could have done about it. And everyone who worked with Ted knew that, too.

Ted's sense of pride would not allow him to take a deep breath and make peace with the changes. He honestly thought that by speaking to his boss's boss he could turn back the clock and return things to the way they were. But he soon discovered he was fighting a losing battle.

THE DANGERS OF LETTING ANGER
GET THE BETTER OF YOU

Ted tried to cool his heels by putting the takeover and firings behind him. But as hard as he tried to bury himself in his work, he couldn't forget the changes. Seeing his boss at meetings and in the corridors triggered his rage. His boss was like a painful thorn in his side. Two months after the reorganization, Ted couldn't take it anymore. He was angrier than ever. He hated his boss and it was gnawing away at him. If his boss at least said he had no choice and was apologetic, Ted would have felt differently. There could have been a foundation for a relationship. But that never happened. His boss showed no regret. In fact, in the months following the reorganization, his boss acted more arrogantly than ever.

Instead of seeing Ted as an asset, his boss bypassed him every chance he could. If he needed input on a project, he sought advice from a junior worker who didn't have Ted's knowledge. The final straw was when Ted wasn't invited to confidential strategic planning sessions that he had previously attended.

Unfortunately, Ted's pride got the better of him and eventually did him in. Viewing the situation as intolerable, he decided to complain to his boss's boss. He could have just thrown in the towel and found another job, but that wasn't Ted's style. He deemed managing his boss and transferring to another department as inadequate solutions.

MAKING ALL THE WRONG MOVES

Late one afternoon, Ted visited his boss's boss and asked if he could have a few words with her in private. She agreed and he closed the door behind him. Ted got straight to the point. He said he came to discuss the problems he was having with his new boss. He said his new boss was unreasonable, belligerent, and yes, unqualified to run an important unit. It was only a matter of time before the company would pay a heavy price for his sloppiness. He didn't stop there. He said it was a mistake giving a lunatic like this so much power and that he wasn't alone in his feelings. Virtually everyone who reported to him felt the same way. For these reasons, he believed the company should take a hard look at the job his boss is doing. Finally, he said that he wanted to report to another senior manager. If not, he'd be forced to hand in his resignation.

TED'S BIGGEST MISTAKES

To say that Ted put the proverbial noose around his neck is an understatement indeed. In the space of a 30-minute conversation, he virtually ended his career with the company, according to management consultant Joe Weintraub, who offers critical advice for going above your boss's head.

- *Consider whether the superior is approachable.* In other words, do you have a sympathetic listener? It's virtually the same advice offered in Chapter Fourteen when considering having a heart-to-heart talk with your boss.

    If Ted had realized he was speaking to a pawn of the new regime, he would have kept his mouth shut. Although his boss's boss had been with the company 8 years, she was still sympathetic with the new regime. An opportunist with an eye on a senior executive slot, she was not to be trusted. Ted never considered that he was not speaking to an impartial source who would act fairly on his behalf. In short, Ted should have stamped her "unapproachable."

- *Don't cast yourself as a martyr.* Here again, Ted struck out. No one wants to feel as if they're being ganged up on. That's a palace coup-type of thinking, warns Weintraub. *Remember:* Companies are not minidemocracies. They're more akin to totalitarian governments run by a small and powerful group. No one cares if you're a spokesperson for the majority of workers. Not only are you making yourself look bad, you're also potentially hurting others who would have preferred it if you kept your mouth shut. Weintraub's best advice: Speak for yourself. "Presenting yourself as a martyr is one of the biggest career-limiting moves you can make," he warns.

- *Don't present ultimatums.*   Ted blew it again when he said that he couldn't take it anymore and was considering leaving. First, he stepped up to the pulpit when he said that it was only a matter of time before the company would pay a heavy price for his boss's sloppiness and primitive management techniques. But the topper was saying that if he didn't report to a new senior manager, he'd be forced to resign.

   How do you think his boss's boss reacted to that threat? You guessed it. Like any seasoned executive who has mastered the game well, she expressed concern. She was so convincing that Ted naively thought she was sympathetic to his cause. When he shook her hand and left, he was convinced positive changes were imminent. He would have been horrified if he knew she chuckled at Ted's naiveté as soon as he closed the door. But the clincher was her call to Ted's boss informing him of the conversation. She expressed dismay over Ted's disloyalty and advised his boss to turn up the heat. Her closing remark was, "I'm very disappointed, but Ted is *just* not a team player."

- *Don't spill all the beans.*   Ted's performance points up the danger of being too honest. Unless it's a life-or-death situation, don't mistakenly make your company an ethical or moral battleground. Of course, companies ought to be fair and honest with their employees. They ought to create healthy environments for their employees. But the truth is that companies exist to turn a profit. In pursuit of that end, many companies use ethical issues, diversity training, and minority recruitment as public relations tools to create a favorable perception. The reasons are obvious. Major food companies, for example, go out of their way to tell the world they hire African-Americans, Latinos, and Asians. Reason? It's not to show how altruistic they are, but simply to sell more canned soup and cereal. Their demographics tell them that a healthy percentage of their customers are minorities. Weintraub's advice: "Don't lose sight of the big picture." See your place in the company realistically. Idealism is fine to a point. After that, it runs smack in the face of naiveté.

As you may have guessed, all of Ted's hard work to right his situation ended in failure. A month after he spoke to his boss's boss, he handed in his resignation and left the company. If he thought his boss was a horror story before he spoke to his boss's boss, he deemed him a dangerous demon after he spilled his guts. Ted's boss turned up the heat to the point where Ted was badly scalded. Rather than find an excuse to fire him, he decided to make Ted's life a living hell.

OPTIMAL CONDITIONS FOR GOING ABOVE YOUR BOSS'S HEAD

PROGRESSIVE CORPORATE CULTURE HELPS

Now that you've seen what not to do, here's how to go above your boss's head and the conditions that make for a good outcome.

Your best ally is a progressive corporate culture, whether real or in principle only. Companies with the budgets to afford large corporate communications departments can afford to promote a corporate culture that will make it look good in the public eye. They'll make a big deal about their recycling efforts, how they spend zillions to clean up the environment, or how they protect endangered species. They'll spare no effort to get the message out. Socially aware companies love flying their "diversity" banner before the public. It usually works. Most people like to read about diversity, even though they're not quite sure what it means. It all comes under the heading of a caring corporate culture.

Cynicism aside, some companies actually do mean what they say. Others just give lip service to the progressive corporate culture credo because it sells products. Bear in mind that many companies actually do put their money where their mouth is and have worker-centered corporate cultures. Naturally, these are the companies where you stand your best shot of calling management on bad behavior. Unless you've got a relative on the board of directors or are related to the CEO, you're not going to easily revolutionize a backward, autocratic corporate culture.

As a general rule, progressive corporate cultures offer the following benefits:

- *Open communication lines.* This means they actually encourage workers to express opinions and dissatisfaction. Weintraub says some companies promote what they call "skip-leveling." Simply, it means employees have the opportunity to talk openly to their boss's boss. The company has an accountability mechanism built into the corporate culture that it views as a creative way to improve morale and productivity simultaneously.

  "Skip-leveling is a marvelous career-building tool," says Weintraub. "Rather than putting their careers on the line, they're actually enhancing them because there is no retribution." Whether your boss's boss actually goes to bat for you and rights a difficult situation or is merely an attentive listener is another issue. However, it's reassuring to know you can speak your mind without being ostracized or canned.

  The bad news is most companies don't have a clue what skip-leveling is all about. Yet Weintraub says the 10-year-old concept is gaining ground thanks to crusading management consultants.

- *Mechanisms that encourage change.* Suggestion boxes have been around for at least a century. Progressive companies have elevated the traditional suggestion box to a new level. In many companies, it's nothing short of a technological instrument of change. While the traditional suggestion box still exists, many companies have created an electronic equivalent. Disgruntled employees can anonymously air their gripes via e-mail. Companies that have adopted electronic suggestion boxes report incredible results. The obvious advantage is employees can fire off an anonymous epistle via their computer from the privacy of their office. Not only does it give management a true reading on the pulse of its workers, but it also acts as a catalyst for change.

Some companies are experimenting with creating impartial intermediaries so workers can complain without fear of reprisal. Usually, they're low-level supervisors who identify with workers more than management because they have worked their way through the ranks. While it sounds great in concept, many workers don't trust the concept of having an impartial spokesperson. And they have good reason to question selfless altruistic acts. Cynical old-timers who have spent time in the trenches have learned that management often can't be trusted. What seems like a genuine act of caring is often a tactic for weeding out troublemakers. And the so-called impartial intermediary is actually a management plant who's working for the corner-office crowd.

However, many progressive companies actually have an open-door policy so workers can vent their frustrations and gripes. Informal and casual atmospheres often encourage honesty and improved communication between management and staff.

Now let's wind down with some tips on the best techniques for confronting your boss.

HOW TO CONFRONT YOUR BOSS'S BOSS: THE PROCESS

By now, you've learned you can't barge into your boss's office and uninhibitedly speak your mind. You saw what happened to Ted. He blew his career chances at the company because he naively thought good wins over evil. Maybe it does if you're the Lone Ranger or Wonder Woman.

Ted had no intention of taking his injustice lying down. He was a self-made man who intended to fight for his beliefs. Unfortunately, it became his cross to bear. One of Ted's biggest shortcomings was that he was a clean fighter. Sadly, that's not always an asset in the business world. If he understood the rules of the game and realized that there are no rules in business, he would have kept his mouth shut.

If you're contemplating confronting your boss, consider these suggestions:

- *Evaluate your chances for success.* If you're walking a dangerous line between success and failure, avoid confronting your boss. If you're walking on hot coals yet have another job in the wings, by all means go for it. No matter what happens, you'll come out ahead. In short, think honestly and rationally about the outcome. It would be wonderful if the good guys always win and ride off victorious into the night. But that's not the way the game is played.

- *Plan out the event as much as possible.* Of course, things seldom go according to plan. Nevertheless, the more thought and planning that go into the event, the better your chances of success. Create an imaginary dialogue with your boss's boss. Imagine both favorable and negative reactions to your observations so you'll be able to respond appropriately.

- *Be descriptive, not evaluative.* When it comes to the actual meeting, Weintraub stresses, "Give information but don't analyze the situation." You need to drive home the fact that you want to improve your performance and your working relationship with your boss.

Early in the conversation, Weintraub suggests saying: "I've tried several times to talk to Marisa, but I don't think it is going anywhere. I'd like to give you some feedback...."

The goal is to create the impression that you want to be helpful and supportive, rather than vindictive. Drive home the idea that the problem is bothering you and affecting your work. Once a solution is found, you'll be a human dynamo, unstoppable and happy in the bargain.

Advice: Instead of using a lot of "we" statements, describe the problem in the first person. You're not a spokesperson for other workers; you're only trying to solve your own problem. "Playing the 'we' card doesn't win a lot of credibility," says Weintraub.

Uppermost, tell your boss's boss you're seeking advice. "Put him or her in a helping- and-coaching-mode rather than in a defensive-mode," adds Weintraub. "Achieve that end and you stand an excellent chance of seeing positive results."

Absolute no-no: Whatever you do, don't back your boss's boss against a wall so that he or she is forced to defend your boss. If that happens, you've batted out with no hope of getting on base.

But if you've diplomatically made your case and the conversation is moving at a relaxed pace, be prepared to offer solutions. In fact, you know you've done a brilliant job if your boss's boss says, "I fully understand the problem, but what do you think we should do about it?" Bingo! Now is your chance to propose solutions. In fact, the more ideas you have, the better.

Finally, as you inch toward the door knowing you turned in an award-winning performance, wind down by putting yourself in the hands of your boss's boss. You might say, "I know you'll do the right thing. I look forward to hearing from you soon. I appreciate your taking the time to listen to me." Say no more. Make a graceful exit and hope for the best.

Hopefully, your boss's boss will do something about the problem. But there is also a good chance he or she will do nothing but discreetly forget your conversation ever happened. And then, of course, there is the remote possibility of a bad outcome. Even though you felt your chances of success were high, your boss's boss pulls a fast one by teaming up with your boss to make your life miserable. Anything can happen. You'd be wise to consider all eventualities.

If you think going over your boss's head is a traumatic move, what do you do if your boss is a crook? Let's find out.

WHAT DO YOU DO WHEN YOUR BOSS IS INVOLVED IN WRONGDOING OR IS A CROOK?

THE DANGERS OF PULLING THE PLUG

Solution Ten: Whistle-blowers almost always jeopardize their careers. Only use this extreme tactic if you have allies in high places.

It happens every day. Whether by design or accident, people learn that their boss is up to no good, and they become bothered enough to do something about it. Take, for example, ousted Texaco senior executive Richard A. Lundwall who pulled the plug on his giant employer a couple of years ago by releasing taped conversations revealing discriminatory hiring and promotion practices that had been going on for years.

To Lundwall's chagrin, this single moral act not only destroyed his career and many long friendships, but it seriously affected his health as well. Looking back, Lundwall harbors deep regret about his actions. If he had to do it again, chances are he would keep his mouth shut, thus avoiding an avalanche of negative publicity.

Lundwall was conflicted about the company's biased hiring practices, but somehow managed to stomach it until the bleak day in June 1996 when he was summoned to an executive vice president's office and told his job would be eliminated. Lundwall was devastated and almost rendered speechless by the news. After 30 years of faithful service, he couldn't understand how they could summarily end his career in the space of a 15-minute conversation.

Like many Texaco veterans, he had seen plenty of friends fired over the years. In fact, he himself had fired his fair share of people. But not in his worst nightmares did he dream it would happen to him. After all, he was the consummate company man and an inspiring success story in his own right. He began his career with Texaco by pumping gas as a service station attendant and rapidly moved up the ladder into management ranks. The company became his life, often coming before his family. Lundwall routinely worked late, giving up weekends and vacations. His three-decade stay at Texaco was a story of self-sacrifice. For Lundwall, being fired was like getting shot by a 12-gauge shotgun at point-blank range.

When he recovered from the devastating blow, he interviewed for other positions in the company, but to no avail. At his angriest low point, he decided to get even by helping minority executives who had been building a discrimination suit since 1994. Lundwall proved a key player in the plaintiff's suit against the multinational company. Like many high-placed Texaco executives, Lundwall had conclusive proof that discriminatory hiring had been going on for years.

If Lundwall thought he had it bad after he was fired, his problems compounded the moment he agreed to help the minority executives. He became the center of an ugly lawsuit that made headlines in newspapers across the United States. Diversity is a big issue these days, and it becomes national news when a Fortune 500 company that promotes itself as an equal-opportunity employer is accused of racism.

When the long drawn-out legal battle finally ended, Lundwall was left permanently scarred. He never considered that Texaco would retaliate with all the firepower it could muster. Not only was its image at stake, but the giant intended to get even with Lundwall for dragging the Texaco name through the mud. Lundwall quickly became humbled when his company cut off his sizable retirement benefits. If he had kept his mouth shut, at least he would have had a secure income for the rest of his life. Now the former executive had to start over, a depressing thought for this self-made man who had been working since he was a teenager. He knew he'd never find another job that would pay him a salary that even faintly approached what he was earning at Texaco.

Would he do it again? He told a *New York Times* reporter, "If I knew what was going to occur, no. In the real world you don't want to put your head in that guillotine."

WHY SPEAK UP?

FROM SEXUAL HARASSMENT TO LIFE-OR-DEATH ISSUES

If it makes you feel better, not all cases end as badly as Lundwall's run-in with Texaco. Most seldom get to the point where they're aired in the press and on the nightly news. Typically, there is a resolution that doesn't end up with the destruction of someone's career.

While justice was served by Lundwall spilling the beans about Texaco's discriminatory hiring practices, his motives were not totally altruistic. Yet, on countless occasions, speaking out is a necessity. The number of sexual harassment cases, for example, has mushroomed over the last few years. After decades of enduring inappropriate and offensive behavior from overbearing bosses, employees have discovered there are legal recourses that can correct the situation without risking the loss of their jobs.

On another level, there are occasions when not speaking out can carry life-or-death implications. Countless times, ethical employees have pulled the plug on bosses who condoned dangerous practices or procedures, such as unsanitary packaging methods, the use of outdated assembly-line equipment, or substandard inspection procedures, to name a few. Because of the problem, lives have been lost and workers have been seriously, even permanently, disfigured.

A few years back, the owner of a multimillion-dollar meat-packing plant was charged with using substandard equipment and implementing inhumane work procedures under which workers had lost fingers and hands because the assembly line was speeded up to increase productivity. During exhausting 4-hour shifts, workers raced to keep up with the assembly line on which they were required to cut cattle with dangerous power tools. One out-of-sync move could cause the line either to slow down or speed up and trigger a bad accident. Making matters worse, the equipment was seldom upgraded or replaced because the boss had been paying off the government inspectors whose job it was to make sure the meat-packing equipment was safe.

In other cases, workers in drug manufacturing plants have reported their bosses for using unsanitary packaging methods. There have even been a couple of cases in which managers at nuclear power plants turned in their senior management for not repairing leaks which not only endangered the lives of workers but also those of millions of residents in the surrounding communities.

When lives are at stake, the obvious question is: Can you afford not to speak up? Could you live with yourself if people were killed because of an accident or disaster caused by something you failed to report? You risk paying a lifelong price for your silence.

THE WORST THAT WILL HAPPEN IS YOU'LL LOSE YOUR JOB

Thankfully, most of us work at jobs where we don't have to report bosses for committing unlawful, immoral, or unethical acts. However, it's good to know that you can speak out without facing retaliatory measures such as having your legs broken or your family threatened. That's precisely what happened in the early 1900s when many powerful robber baron entrepreneurs ran companies with an iron fist. (I'll explore this slice of Americana in more depth in the appendix.) Suffice it to say that not too long ago you could actually put your life in danger by speaking out against your boss.

Today, fortunately, the worst that could happen is you risk getting fired. In some emancipated companies, even that's rare. IBM and a few other blue-chip companies actually encourage employees to bring up complaints so they can be investigated, with the accuser remaining anonymous. Others make a point of saying there will be no retaliation for speaking out against an injustice, whether it relates to a company policy or a deviant boss.

Warning: Be wary of company hype. Know what's fact and what's public relations fiction. Many big companies that depend on a spotless image to sell products will try to milk diversity and environmental issues for all they are worth. But whether they practice what they preach is another matter. It's up to you to find out. The same applies to mechanisms for reporting wrongdoing.

Most of us have been taught to protect our bosses. That's a carryover from the days when companies actually guaranteed lifetime employment, and loyal workers held one job for their entire career. In the face of more than 15 years of corporate downsizing, job security is part of a bygone era.

YOU DON'T HAVE TO PUT YOUR JOB ON THE LINE

You Can Speak Out and Win— If You Do It Properly

If you're going to speak out, here are some tips for doing it properly:

- *Gauge the playing field.* Evaluate the level of risk and possible outcomes. Know what you're getting into from the onset. Even under the best circumstances, it's impossible to predict the outcome. Don't attempt to be a hero at a traditional or conservative company that promotes and protects its managers. Your chances will be similarly slim at tightly controlled family-run companies. Their unwritten credo is almost always: "Protect family members at all cost." You stand your best chances at liberated, well-managed, large and mid-sized companies with a history of promoting employee welfare, enrichment, and empowerment programs.

Many national business magazines such as *Fortune, Forbes,* and *INC.* have done exhaustive stories about liberated companies that have supported workers' rights and stood behind the courageous workers who had the guts to report a wrongdoing. If you have access to the Internet, these stories can be accessed easily by loading the home page of a search engine (such as Infoseek, Yahoo!, or MetaCrawler) and typing in the words "corporate whistle-blowers." You'll be pleasantly surprised to uncover hundreds of articles on the subject.

You expect large companies to support employee rights, but there are also plenty of small liberated companies run by emancipated MBAs where real change is taking place.

- *Rally the troops.* If the environment is right for speaking up against a corrupt boss, don't do it alone. Gather a support team. There is great truth in the cliché, "There is strength in numbers." First, the battle could get bloody, so it pays to have troops supporting you throughout the tough period. And second, the more support you have, the better your chances of succeeding. Management and the public won't just see a lone disgruntled whistle-blower seeking revenge, but instead will see workers fighting an injustice.

- *Play by the rules.* Don't be naive and think a boss accused of wrongdoing won't retaliate. Remember what happened to Lundwall at Texaco. The former executive never anticipated the devastating fusillade that destroyed his retirement by wiping out his pension benefits. A simple rule of thumb: The more powerful the boss, the longer the battle and the dirtier the tactics. To protect a company's tarnished image, don't think a company wouldn't sue you. This is why it's imperative you keep accurate records of your every move. It's also critical that you play by the rules. In fact, the cleaner you play, the better your chances of success. If there are protocols for filing complaints and reporting wrongdoing, follow them to the letter. Document every step of the battle. If the potential case involves embezzlement, stealing, or life-or-death issues where employees or customers are in danger, make multiple copies of notes and correspondence and make sure your attorney has a complete file. The more diligent you are about guarding and carefully chronicling your evidence, the better your chances of winning.

- *Listen to your gut and play hunches.* There is no logic to following instinct and listening to unexplainable gut feelings. I simply urge you to do it. If something doesn't feel right or if you have a strange premonition about making a certain move, heed your inner voice. You may pat yourself on the back in the end.

Finally, a last word of advice. *Be careful!* Calling a boss on wrongdoing is serious stuff. Proceed with the utmost caution.

While you're in a fighting mood, the next chapter offers tips for telling off your boss. Why not put the noose around your neck and get some sweet revenge at the same time?

SWEET REVENGE: "TAKE THIS JOB AND SHOVE IT."

THE PROS AND CONS OF TELLING OFF YOUR BOSS

Solution Eleven: Getting even by quitting and telling your boss off is a dangerous tactic that's discouraged under all circumstances. Only consider this tactic if there is no threat of reprisal.

If Johnny Paycheck predicted what damage his popular hit song "Take This Job and Shove It" would have wrought on America's working masses, he would have thought twice about releasing it. It fulfilled every workingperson's fantasy. Paycheck crystallized all our feelings about the bosses we've hated and the joys of telling this loathsome person exactly how we feel. He struck a universal chord.

Thousands of disgruntled workers have taken Paycheck's advice and told their bosses what to do with their jobs. Initially, there were delicious feelings of sweet revenge. But then reality reared its omnipotent head. Like a thundercloud hanging over the heads of these workers, the future suddenly looked bleak. They wondered whether it was worth it.

Most of the people I spoke with who told off their bosses now regret it and admit it was an impulsive decision made without considering the repercussions.

THE DANGERS OF LOSING YOUR COOL

Consider what happened to a journalist buddy who worked closely with me on a Sunday supplement. I was the editor, he was the managing editor, and we both reported to a tyrannical publisher who deserved to spend the rest of his days in a straightjacket. The publisher was an old-school martinet who insisted upon doing things his way. Unfortunately, his way was usually the wrong way. But it was impossible to convince this burned-out relic that there was a better way to do things, especially if suggested by someone younger and smarter. That would have meant acknowledgment of his ignorance and his need to learn from a subordinate. My friend and I knew our boss would never experience that kind of revelatory epiphany.

With a good deal of deep-breathing exercises, not to mention frequent beers after work, I managed to stomach my boss. More important, I managed to coexist with this person. I reasoned that if I locked horns with him, I'd be arguing with him all day long and nothing would ever get done. When it came down to the wire, my responsibility was to meet my deadlines and get the paper out on schedule. My solution was to get him out of my hair by yessing him to death and then spinning on my heels and doing as I pleased.

My friend found that tactic offensive and continued to lock horns with him. Not a day went by when they didn't have at least one bad argument. Sometimes, they verbally sparred all day long. Around deadlines, especially, the tension was so thick you could cut it with a knife. And needless to say, it made everyone nervous. The tension became so bad that the publisher challenged practically everything my friend said. The issue of right and wrong was no longer important.

In short, the two men hated each other. At its core was not so much a personality dispute but a generational conflict. The older man felt intimidated and challenged by the smart, feisty editor 35 years his junior. And my friend was incensed that he had to take orders from a loudmouthed moron who should have retired a decade ago.

Then it happened. To this day, my friend wishes he could have rewritten his life's script. It was just before Christmas, a typically hectic time for newspapers. Increased ad revenues translated into more editorial pages and longer hours for everyone. This is when astute management is critical. For my friend, who was responsible for coordinating advertising and editorial schedules, it was a living hell. The lunatic publisher kept on demanding that closings be extended in order to squeeze the last penny out of advertisers. But it also meant pushing back editorial schedules, which could throw off the entire publishing machine. In a word, it meant chaos. One busy day at 8 p.m., when we were all exhausted from working 12 straight hours, the publisher barged into my friend's office ordering him to delay closing an issue an extra day because he was expecting a big ad from a beverage company. That was the last straw as far as my friend was concerned.

Until then, he had worked hard at respectfully disagreeing with our boss. Tired, stressed, and pushed to the limit, he couldn't take it anymore. The publisher was asking for the impossible, and my friend was not about to alter the entire printing schedule for an additional $5000 in ad income. He told the publisher he wasn't going to do it and that he was through taking orders from a "tired old washed-out incompetent who should be running a garment factory rather than publishing a newspaper." He didn't stop there. He unleashed a string of nasty expletives, which good taste dictates I leave out of this text, and ranted insults at the older man for 15 minutes. The outburst was unplanned and spontaneous. Even worse, it happened in our large editorial bullpen where everyone heard the fireworks.

My friend was relentless and kept on attacking the publisher where it hurt the most, about his age and incompetence. One of the last things my friend said was, "Why don't you give us all a break, get out of the business, and move to a retirement community in Florida? You won't be able to do any damage then."

Throughout the entire tirade, the stunned publisher quietly

watched my friend rant and rave. Just when he was about finished, the publisher told my friend he'd made the biggest mistake of his career. My friend returned with, "I don't think so. I just saved my life. I can't work for a jerk like you for another second. Find another managing editor. I quit."

GETTING THE LAST LAUGH

Through it all, the publisher kept his composure. Once my friend finished talking, he returned with, "Now I'm going to have the last word. I'd like to see you in my office immediately." In this highly charged emotional situation, my friend found himself in the publisher's office.

Our boss may not have been the brightest publisher, but he certainly had an appetite for tactful revenge. Rather than continuing to make the argument a public event, he started playing the authority figure by demanding a private meeting, which quickly reaffirmed his position. If he had remained there bickering with my friend, he would have lost all credibility. Like a judge banning TV cameras from the courtroom, our boss turned the conflict between my friend and himself into a private matter. The boss suddenly went up a notch in our estimation, proving he wasn't the fool we all thought he was.

As soon as he got the younger man in his office, he mercilessly unloaded both barrels. In the quiet of the boss's office, the older man firmly reestablished his authority. My friend just sat and listened. Hardly 15 minutes before, he had sounded his own death knell. Now the boss read him his last rites.

In plain English, the boss said his editor had crossed the line by violating all the rules of good taste. He told him that he had made a big mistake by quitting. Despite working for the newspaper for 5 years, he eliminated his entitlement to unemployment insurance. What's more, the boss pledged to do everything in his power to make sure my friend had a difficult time withdrawing his pension fund allotment. Legally, he couldn't prevent him from getting it, but he could certainly slow up the paperwork.

That's just for starters. The publisher told the editor he intended to put the word out to every newspaper in the city that my friend is a hot-tempered loose cannon who can't handle pressure and should not work in the high-stress newspaper industry where cool heads and calm personalities are critical. Naturally, like any vindictive boss, he planned on casting himself as a wronged supervisor who tried his best to deal with an impossible situation.

Within 24 hours of my friend's emotional outburst, the boss had e-mailed the publisher of every newspaper in the city and followed this up with a signed letter, leaving a paper trail. In his scorching denouncement of my friend, the publisher altered the facts in his favor. Instead of saying that my friend quit, he reframed the facts and said that irrational, irresponsible behavior, compounded by a series of costly decisions, forced him to fire him despite a treacherous deadline.

Not only did the publisher get revenge, he also besmirched my friend's professional reputation. There was little question the younger man acted irrationally and tactlessly. However, his professional performance had been flawless and commendable. In the face of the worst possible working conditions, my friend always managed to make good decisions. In fact, he was one of the best managing editors I've ever known. Like many seasoned newspaper professionals, he thrived under pressure. Unfortunately, few people will ever know he had to work under horrible conditions with an incompetent boss who'd be in bankruptcy court if not for an experienced staff who kept the publication afloat.

The publisher did everything he could think of to get even. He told the newspaper community that my friend lacked the essential attributes of a seasoned journalist: reliability, competence, accuracy, and most crucial, consistent performance under duress. He made sure he'd never get a staff job on any daily newspaper within the entire city. Unless he moved to another city, his only job options were a magazine job or, worse yet, writing press releases for a public relations firm, an embarrassing comedown after working for a prestigious newspaper.

Need I say more? You can translate the foregoing scenario to virtually any industry or job situation. More important, priceless advice can be extracted from this real-life saga.

ANALYSIS: PAYING THE PRICE

Few people who tell off their bosses consider the price they may have to pay for a few moments of revenge. They should consider the following facts:

- *The boss might retaliate.* Like wounded animals, many despotic bosses will go to extensive lengths to ruin a former employee's reputation.
- *The boss might lie or alter the facts to ruin the reputation or destroy the credibility of the employee who quit.* Many bosses have actually used the phrase, "As long as I'm alive, I'm going to do everything in my power to make sure you never work in this town again." And many of them meant it.
- *A crazed boss will go to any length to get revenge.* If your boss is normally erratic, unpredictable, hot-tempered, irrational, or given to bursts of odd behavior, how do you think he or she will act when crossed, provoked, or pushed to the limit?

Take my friend's case. The younger man never imagined the publisher would lie and try to ruin his reputation. My friend waged an unwinnable war. Although he's smart and talented, the publisher is in the power seat. Naturally, some people will question the facts, but my friend was put in the indelicate position of having to clear his reputation and explain himself. Many publishers won't even question information from another publisher. Every industry has a power chain. Publishers guard the bottom line and are considered more important than reporters and editors. Thus, they have more credibility.

CAN WE REPLAY THAT SCENE?

FOUR CARDINAL RULES OF CAREER BUILDING

1. *Pocket your anger.*   Bridge burning is a poor choice. Needless to say, my friend regrets his emotional outburst. Unfortunately, he can't retract what he said in the heat of anger. Many people I spoke to who have told off their bosses wish they had pocketed their rage and kept their mouths shut. The majority never thought about the repercussions. Bridge burning is always a bad idea.

2. *Never leave a job until you have another one to replace it.* This commandment of job searching can be traced to the beginning of time, yet millions of people ignore it. Smart job seekers leverage their job experience. Regardless of the circumstances, most potential employers will consider you more valuable if you're still employed. As soon as you join the ranks of the unemployed, you lose valuable negotiating points. Employers ask a very obvious question: Why doesn't this person have a job?

3. *Never underestimate the power of a wronged boss.*   What would you do if you were a boss and an employee berated and insulted you? Worse yet, what if the employee had the temerity to do it publicly? I'd want to get even in some way. For some, the thirst for revenge gets downright ugly. Many wronged bosses don't stop until they've ruined an employee's career.

4. *Sometimes it pays to wait out a bad situation.*   It's not easy to take a deep breath and wait till things get better. But events or circumstances beyond your control often right themselves. If you stick around long enough, you could outlast your boss. I'm not suggesting that you wait a

decade for your boss to get out of your hair, but bosses are transferred, take other jobs, retire, die, or are even fired, a thought that always draws a satisfied smile. If the stars are right, you may not have to leave the company. You may even wind up with your boss's job. Now there's a concept you never considered. What kind of boss will you be? Will you be an improvement on your boss or just as vicious, vindictive, and evil as he or she was? Obviously, you can't answer those questions until you are cast in that role.

THE BEST SITUATIONS FOR TELLING OFF YOUR BOSS

One thing is certain. There is no optimal scenario for telling your boss where to go. The best you can hope for is doing so under decent conditions. They include the following:

- *Switching to a new industry.* It's the equivalent of moving to a new place and starting over. In this era of job hopping and career changing, it's very common to apply your skills in a new industry. Bosses are not omniscient. Thankfully, their reign of terror is confined to one industry. Once you've crossed industry lines, a former boss's power and influence suddenly disappear.

- *Your boss has a long history of abuse.* Some bad bosses are legends within their industry. In situations like this, their reputation precedes them. Telling off your boss could elevate you to hero status. You might draw comments like, "Good for you. It's a wonder more people in that division don't tell that lunatic where to go."

- *You're financially secure and are about to retire.* If you're into the finale of your career and are about to leave your job to do all the things you've dreamed about doing, go for it and tell your demon boss where to go. If you've bottled your rage for many years and played the controlled bureaucrat too long, give yourself some deserved satisfaction. If you're about to retire and have enough stashed away to live out the rest of your life in comfort, why not go out with a bang? Your boss can't hurt you.

- *You have another job and your new boss is supportive.* This is a power position, especially if you have the support of your new boss. Other than an occasional nightmare, there is little your old boss can do to harm you.

- *Your boss is about to retire.* Caution is still advised. If your boss was a known demon, it doesn't matter what you say to him or her. But if your boss still has friends in high places and is still going to play a role in your company, possibly in a consulting capacity or on the board of directors, think twice about getting even. Even though he won't be physically present, his influence can still be felt.

CONSIDER THE FUTURE

QUIT WITH HONOR

The best advice is to consider the future before you act out Johnny Paycheck's tune. Ask yourself what damage will be incurred by telling off your boss. What will happen to your career, reputation, and credibility?

It's not easy stifling your anger if you've been stomaching a lunatic for 50 weeks a year. Nevertheless, I encourage you to try.

If you must confront your boss, do it discreetly. Avoid public displays of anger. Speak to your boss privately and try to stick to the issues at hand. Even though your boss has made your life miserable and has used every unsavory tactic in the book, don't stoop to his or her level. Avoid name-calling, screaming, ranting, and even though you may want to hurl the bane of your existence out the window, resist physical violence. Play it clean and quit with honor. You'll applaud your self-control later. Don't let your boss have the last laugh.

ALL-PURPOSE STRATEGIES FOR GETTING ON WITH NEW, INDECISIVE, DELEGATOR, AND OTHER GARDEN VARIETY BOSSES

Solution Twelve: Only flexible chameleons will succeed with the most difficult bosses. Make no assumptions about your work environment, especially the people you're going to be working with closely. Be ready to adapt to a changing working landscape.

The folks who climbed the corporate ladder are true survivalists. Some were lucky, others just happened to be in the right place at the right time, but the majority had the right constitution and attitude for success. Their thinking went something like this: "I'll get on with everybody, even insane and incompetent bosses. I'm not going to let anyone stand in my way." The rest of the working masses allow their environments to do them in.

Let's wind down with all-purpose strategies for getting along with the bosses we deal with all the time. These are not the wackos detailed earlier, but the commonplace-to-difficult ones we must get on with to build our careers.

Let's take it from the top and find out how to make a positive impression with a new boss.

SCORE POINTS WITH A NEW BOSS

In the past, the majority of workers had two to three jobs in their lifetime. Many worked for one company, which often meant reporting to one boss for most of their career. If you moved up through the ranks, it meant scoring points with a couple of bosses. Yet, remaining in one company usually made it easier to adjust to your workplace and excel at your work.

Bosses were replaced when they retired, died, were promoted, or transferred. Today, having many bosses is common. And the reasons are all of the above plus frequent takeovers, mergers, acquisitions, and reorganizations.

Unlike the past, where each boss had his or her own special agenda which usually meant bringing in new talent and undertaking new projects, new bosses are usually brought in to tighten the organization so it's leaner, meaner, and more profitable.

Even though the worst of corporate downsizing is over, it's still taking place. Each month, the U.S. Bureau of Labor Statistics releases new "separation" figures, revealing companies' obsession with discarding excess human baggage. Bottom-line thinking says each employee must carry his or her own weight. Many companies have gone to great lengths to keep their payrolls as lean as possible. If there is a way to outsource by using consultants, temps, or contract workers, companies will jump at the opportunity to pare operating costs.

Keep these facts of business life in mind if you have to score points with a new boss. Most new bosses bring an agenda with them which reads: Get things done quickly, efficiently, and cheaply.

FIRST IMPRESSIONS COUNT

What with rapid turnover and constant corporate overhauls and reorganizations, if you've been with a company for more than 5 years, chances are you've had your fair share of new bosses. Depending on how they stack up with your former boss, they probably rated from good to atrocious. Whether you like or detest them, you have no choice but to get along with them.

Whether you've inherited a demon or a saint, if you're smart you'll start off on the right foot by making a great first impression. How you make that initial favorable impression depends on your circumstances and the personal chemistry between you and your boss.

BACK OFF AND LET YOUR NEW BOSS GET THE LAY OF THE LAND

Some management consultants recommend what they call the "proactive approach." Rather than waiting for your boss to tell you what he or she wants, they advise knocking on his or her door and making your presence known by offering a helping hand. Before he knows where the restrooms are located, you're offering to be his seeing-eye dog.

This is a presumptuous tactic which I don't recommend. Strategic career builders have the good sense to back off and allow their new bosses breathing room so they can get the lay of the land. Building relationships with staffers is often not an immediate priority, a fact of company life that many narcissistic overachievers can't fathom.

More important issues for many new bosses include meeting with their bosses to find out what's expected of them and getting a feeling for corporate protocol. After that, it's learning about who does what and figuring out how to get things done. When all that is accomplished, it's time to sit down with the troops in order to get down to the mission at hand.

Most new bosses sort out all this introductory protocol within the first 3 to 5 days on the job. Companies don't appreciate long start-up periods for either workers or bosses. As one human resources person from a Fortune 500 company put it, "If you can't get yourself together and straighten out your priorities within the first week on the job, it's doubtful you're going to last. We have no time for handholding."

WAIT FOR THE SOP MEETING

Once many new bosses figure out how things work, they schedule a meeting with their employees to explain what Lyle Sussman, coauthor with Sam Deep of *Smart Moves: 14 Steps to Keep Any Boss Happy* (Addison-Wesley), calls standard operating procedure (SOP). "It's a common practice in many companies," he says. "The new boss simply spells out his philosophy and communicates his style and expectations. Usually, they're very brief meetings. It's as basic as this-is-who-I-am, this-is-what-I-believe, and this-is-how-I-want-things-done."

The SOP meetings are also an opportunity for bosses to get to know staffers and for staffers to ask questions and get a better sense of where their boss is coming from. Sussman deems these SOP meetings a positive start. "They eliminate all anxiety for staffers because they know exactly what to expect from their boss," he says. "They don't have to waste time and energy trying to figure out what their boss wants and what it takes to keep this person off their backs."

While SOP meetings are ideal starting points for building a healthy working relationship between bosses and employees, many bosses don't hold these critical briefing meetings. It simply doesn't occur to many new bosses. Then what?

Don't panic. Often, it's nothing to worry about, says Sussman. "If no meeting is conducted and the boss gives you signals that nothing will change and it's business as usual, then continue doing what you've been doing. Don't make it an issue."

However, if you pick up signals or vibrations that things aren't quite right, it's time to sit down with your boss and find out what's on his or her mind before things get worse. The strongest signal, says Sussman, is "tension in the air." "It's hard to describe, yet it's something you feel. I compare it to sensing a pending storm about to erupt."

Advice: If you sense tension or negative vibrations, Sussman and other business consultants urge acting quickly. "Things can get very bad very fast," Sussman asserts. The goal is try to find out if there is anything you're doing that is rubbing your boss the wrong way.

MANAGE EXPECTATIONS

"IF YOU DON'T TALK TO ME, HOW AM I GOING TO KNOW WHAT YOU WANT?"

Communication is the key that opens the door to a good relationship with a new boss who doesn't know how to ask for what he or she wants. If your boss can't communicate with you, you must communicate with him. You have to be prepared to take the first step.

"If your boss doesn't communicate expectations, it can lead to disappointment by both you and your boss," explains Stephen Gilliland, an organizational consultant and associate professor of management and policy at the University of Arizona, Tucson. "Your boss will be disappointed in your performance and you, in turn, will be disappointed because your boss has no idea what you are doing and what you would like to accomplish. Both parties are frustrated with each other."

While Gilliland concedes most bosses are poor communicators, he also observes that most employees are afraid to ask for feedback. The reasons are fear of rejection and negative criticism.

Advice: Recognizing that poor or no communication could be a major stumbling block in your relationship with your new boss, nip the problem in the bud by sitting down with him or her and discussing expectations. Don't wait for your boss to take the first step. "Communicating expectations is a low priority for most bosses and for new bosses it's hardly a consideration because all their time and energy is consumed with adjusting to their job," says Gilliland.

THE PERSONAL MEETING

"INFORMAL" AND "CASUAL" ARE THE OPERATIVE WORDS

During a quiet time of the day, maybe after lunch or late afternoon, ask if you can have a few minutes of your boss's time. "Casual" and "informal" are the operative words. If your boss returns with a brusk, "What's on your mind, Fred?" you return with a low key, "I'd like to tell you what I do and find out a little about your expectations. It would help me greatly in my job."

That gentle introduction should set the tone for a relaxed conversation. Consider this sample presentation by a worker to his boss:

> I don't know whether you got a chance to peruse my records or PAs [performance appraisals]. But allow me to give you a brief description of what I do and what I'm trying to accomplish. I've been with the company for 4 years. I started as a copy intern when I was a senior in college. When I graduated, I was asked to join the company as a copywriter assistant and was assigned to three cosmetics accounts. I reported to the senior copywriter on each of these accounts. It was a great experience because I learned agency fundamentals from three bosses, each of whom gave me a different perspective. I was promoted to junior copywriter 2 years later on the Gex-X Cosmetics and Hurley Perfume accounts. That's what I've been doing ever since. I've been specializing in print, but I am anxious to do TV work as well. I'd like to be able to write for both mediums. When you see some of the ads I've written over the last 2 years, I think you'll agree they've gotten leaner and more focused. Also, the hooks are more polished. My goal is to be promoted to senior copywriter and be totally responsible for one account. I'm ready and I would like to prove that to you. I've been concentrating on every detail of the copy preparation process just short of account management. I eagerly seek out criticism from not only my supervisors but my peers as well. Is there anything else I should be doing?

Analysis: On a scale of 1 to 100, what score would you give this employee? I'd give him a 95. Maybe he didn't have to present a synopsis of his work history with the company, but he managed to strike all the right chords. His tone and attitude were both on the money.

Here's what he did right: His approach was nonconfrontational. It wasn't, "Hey, what's your problem? I'm doing a great job. How come you can't see it?" He didn't put his boss on the defensive. Instead, he said, in effect, "I need some guidance and input. I care very much about my job and my career and I want to know if I'm on the right track. If not, what can I do to veer back onto the right path?"

In short, this employee had the good sense to put himself in his boss's hands. By doing so, he had the courage to open himself up to criticism, a posture other workers might avoid.

In sum, this worker made himself, rather than his boss, the focus of the conversation. From the onset, he never crossed the power line. He respected his boss's position and authority without being obsequious or fawning.

You can't help but win with an approach like that. Even tough-skinned bosses will soften under this approach. Five minutes into the conversation, the boss will see you're an ally rather than an adversary. Even under ideal conditions, when the company is expanding aggressively and profits are high, new bosses need all the help they can get.

This worker has done a great job of ingratiating himself into his boss's good graces. That translates to big points when promotions are doled out.

KEEP THE COMMUNICATION LINES OPEN

If the meeting with your new boss goes well, take advantage of your good fortune by keeping the communication lines open. Rather than making it a one-shot conversation, ask for permission to keep the dialogue going. You might say, "Would it be possible to schedule a monthly feedback session? It would help me a great deal. I can keep you abreast of what projects I'm working on and where I'm headed."

Chances are your boss will welcome the idea. He or she might return with, "It sounds good to me. I think we could both benefit from the chat." End of story.

While new bosses require more of your attention, bosses who've been with the company for many years still have to be managed. Following are some more tips for coping with difficult bosses.

INDECISIVE BOSSES

"WHAT, ME MAKE A DECISION?"

Outsiders find indecisive bosses hard to uncover because they're artists at covering their inadequacies. They also deserve high marks in the self-awareness category. It's their knowledge of their own ineptitude that drives them to take credit for the work of others.

Talented workers, especially, are an indecisive boss's passport to career longevity. As long as they surround themselves with bright, self-assured underlings, they're safe. No one but their staff ever really knows about their deficiencies. Naturally, they're not about to pull the plug on their boss and risk losing their job.

On closer scrutiny, indecisive bosses are easy to spot. Their insecurity gives them away. Whether it's stupidity or fear of making a decision, they'll find a way to avoid it. Even in crisis situations, they'll cleverly find a way to avoid putting a noose around their neck. They'll feign sickness, invent a family crisis, take a vacation day, or schedule a business trip to remove themselves from the situation. But they'll find a way to call upon an intelligent subordinate to make the decision and will take full credit for that decision.

Similarly, indecisive bosses are reluctant to sign off on anything controversial that might cast them in a negative light. They'll go to elaborate lengths to avoid a risky situation. Once again, they'll consult with bright subordinates to find out how to handle the situation. In fact, indecisive bosses have been known to call subordinates at home to pick their brains. A securities analyst employed by a brokerage house said he felt like his boss's confidential adviser:

> In the 6 years I've reported to her, I have never known her to make an important decision by herself. Frightened and insecure, she relies on three senior staffers to make big decisions. Whenever she's in dire straits, she has a knack for finding me. She has no compunction about calling me at any hour. One summer, I was vacationing at a remote cabin on a lake. Mistakenly, I gave my boss my telephone number for emergencies. I never thought she'd actually call. I was wrong. One night she called me at 11 p.m. because she was summoned to an emergency strategy meeting scheduled for the following morning and didn't have a clue what suggestions to offer. It was pathetic. I could hear the tension in her voice. She picked my brain for a half hour before she had enough ideas to make a good impression.

ANALYSIS: COPING STRATEGIES

Indecisive bosses are human parasites. On one hand, they're a sad bunch because they'll do anything to avoid making decisions. On the other hand, they can be manipulative and are not to be trusted. They'll go to great lengths to keep high-performing subordinates close to them at all times. George Fuller, author of *The Workplace Survival Guide* (Prentice Hall), warns that indecisive bosses are reluctant to give star performers good performance appraisals. Says Fuller, "Before you sit down for a performance evaluation with an indecisive boss, rest assured your performance evaluation will be mediocre. This is because an indecisive boss will be reluctant to lose a good worker by way of a promotion." Fuller also notes that indecisive bosses are not beyond downplaying your contributions in public.

Advice: Watch your back. Do not underestimate the self-protective skills of indecisive bosses. They'll go to elaborate extremes to protect their position.

If you hope to move up the ladder and advance your career, the two obvious options are transferring to a new department or finding another job. In either scenario, you'd best keep a record of your accomplishments so you can move quickly when opportunity knocks. The good news is that your indecisive boss has given you incredible opportunities to spotlight your talents. Be prepared to document them when given the chance.

Until you make your move, stay out of your indecisive boss's way. Whatever you do, don't make the mistake of confiding in him or her. Most important, build allies within the company and make sure senior management knows about your accomplishments. The more support you have, the easier it will be to get away from your indecisive boss.

DELEGATOR BOSSES

"WHY MAKE A DECISION WHEN I CAN HAVE SOMEONE ELSE DO IT FOR ME?"

A close cousin of the indecisive boss is the delegator boss. Delegator bosses can be a mixed blessing. Because they lack the ability to organize their workload and get things done, they delegate to others. One worker referred to them as "dumpers." Delegator bosses will mercilessly delegate work to save their jobs. The more pressured they feel, the more they delegate.

The flip side is the more work you take off your boss's incompetent hands, the better your chances of taking over his or her job. Don't underestimate the power of senior management. No matter how well entrenched your boss is, companies have no compunction about discarding dead weight. Justice may one day be served, and you stand to come out ahead.

Fuller notes that there are several pitfalls to working for a delegator boss:

- *The boss doesn't communicate what is expected of you.* Don't expect to get a lot of input from a delegator boss. The longer you work for one, the better you become at filling in the blanks. Make your life easy by plying your boss with questions so you know how to satisfy his or her objectives.

- *You don't have time to do all the work the boss is delegating.* Often, delegator bosses will give assignments to the best workers in the department, according to Fuller. If you don't think you can complete a task because you're overloaded with your own work, let the boss know this fact when the task is assigned. The boss will either be forced to assign the work elsewhere or allow you to complete it at your own speed.

- *You're not given adequate resources to do the job.* Delegator bosses have a knack for assigning projects without providing necessary resources, be it people or equipment. To avoid problems, let the boss know, preferably in writing, what you need to complete a project properly. "If the resources aren't furnished, then you're off the hook for not completing the task," says Fuller.

- *The boss asks you to do a job that makes you unpopular.* Delegator bosses often assign dirty jobs that can make you look bad in front of coworkers and managers. Gracefully decline by saying you're burdened with too much work. If there is no way to get out of it, Fuller suggests quietly using the grapevine to spread the word that you were assigned the job against your wishes. This way, you don't look bad.

- *The boss doles out horrible jobs to you.* Be careful. Many delegator bosses look for easy targets to delegate the worst jobs. Once you accept a terrible job, count on being saddled with it for as long as you report to this person. Avoid problems by declining grunt jobs as soon as they're assigned. Possible excuses? "I've got too much on my plate." If that fails, try honesty: "I find this task unpleasant and beneath me. My talents would be better applied to more challenging projects." I doubt if you'll be fired, but you could be ignored or, better yet, transferred to another department.

- *There is no pleasing the boss.* No matter what you do or

how hard you try, there is no pleasing this person. Fuller points out that if the boss was a true perfectionist, the work wouldn't have to be delegated in the first place. Once again, choices must be made. Do you grin and bear it and wait for better opportunities to present themselves or lose your cool in a moment of anger and tell your incompetent boss where to go? I suggest taking deep breaths and following the former strategy.

- *Your boss takes credit for your successes but blames you for his failures.* You can't win. Your successes are his successes but your failures are your demerits. It sounds worse than it is. But don't underestimate other people's reading of the situation. Delegator bosses ultimately fashion their own nooses. Says Fuller, "Although you may not be getting credit for your good work, everyone else, including other managers, knows where the credit belongs."

BULLY BOSSES

"DO WHAT YOU'RE TOLD OR FIND ANOTHER JOB"

Finally, there are obnoxious bully bosses. They rule by intimidation, insist on getting their way, and fly off the handle easily. They have little concern for other people's feelings. They also treat subordinates as children and seldom ask for anyone's input.

Solutions? Tactful manipulation yields stunning results. Don't become a victim of your boss's madness. If that happens, you're doomed. Sussman and Deep suggest studying your boss's behavior to fashion an avoidance strategy. Resist the temptation to engage your bully boss in a verbal battle. No matter what you say, you'll lose because he or she holds all the power. If you decide to confront your bully boss, "indicate how her behavior is endangering her success," advise authors Sussman and Deep. "Without challenging, threatening, moralizing, or judging, talk about how the behavior is lowering morale and productivity." Here's what you can say: "I find it difficult to excel under circumstances where I am pressured by more than my work, where I am unable to predict moods, and where I'm not trusted. As a result, the work of my unit declines."

It's time to wind down. I've only scratched the surface, and it would take 500 more pages to do the subject justice. I've covered enough ground to give you the ammunition to deal with most crazy bosses. The important message is that you're not alone and are not to blame for your boss's bizarre behavior. First, you must understand the dynamics of the situation and then take action. Whatever you decide to do, your ultimate goal should be to advance your career. Don't let crazy bosses stand in your way. Instead, see them as steppingstones to a higher achievement. If you don't, you're destined to wallow in mediocrity.

THE NOBLE ART
OF MAKING YOUR
BOSS LOOK GOOD

Solution Thirteen: A surefire route to scoring career points is by looking for opportunities that make your boss look good.

Let's wind down with some critical advice that you ought to memorize. Making your boss look good sounds like an obsequious request. I only recommend this strategy if it doesn't compromise your values. Naturally, there are caveats. I'm not suggesting you do something immoral or unethical. As I said earlier, if your boss is involved in wrongdoing and your values are being violated, it's your responsibility to do something about it.

I'm going to make the assumption your boss resides in that gray middle ground where most crazy bosses fall. If so, a highly recommended strategy is to make your boss look good as the opportunities arise. That doesn't mean being a teacher's pet or, the most despicable role of all, your boss's informant. It simply means watching your boss's back and making him or her look good whenever possible. Do it subtly, keep a low profile, and you'll be rewarded.

WARNING! THE WALLS HAVE EARS

Watch what you say about your boss. Even if you have a great working relationship, it's only natural to sound off when you have a complaint or are upset about the way he or she handled a situation. It's human nature to gripe, even about idyllic situations.

But complaining about your boss to a coworker can backfire. Even trusted coworkers have been known to slip and say the wrong thing to the wrong person.

Advice: Never criticize your boss openly at work. If you have to gripe, try confiding in your priest, bartender, or spouse. These confidants won't get you into trouble.

WHAT DOES MAKING YOUR BOSS LOOK GOOD MEAN?

Making a boss look good means supporting this person so that his or her position is secure. In doing so, you're enhancing your own career prospects. Here are ways to make your boss look good:

- *Cover for your boss.*   There'll be times when your boss wants to duck out early for a game of racquetball, to pick up the kids, or simply to beat the rush-hour traffic. Be careful! Making up a lie could backfire for both you and your boss. Let's say a senior manager stops by your desk at 4:30 p.m. on a Friday and asks for your boss. Saying he is at a meeting or with a client is not recommended. The reason is they're obvious lies that can be verified and cause a great deal of embarrassment.

  What should you say to protect your boss? Simply respond, "I don't know." It's a safe lie that won't cause you any grief. Realistically, it's not your responsibility to keep track of your boss's comings and goings.

- *Complement your boss's weaknesses.*   Even supertalented bosses have weak areas. No one can do everything perfectly. It's to your advantage to discover your boss's deficiencies and help him or her in these areas. If done properly and subtly, your boss will willingly unload headaches and frustrating chores. You might say, "John, I noticed you've been busy preparing the monthly sales reports. I'd like to pitch in if you don't mind. I used to take care of that at my last job and I'm familiar with software that can cut the preparation time in half." With an offer like that, I doubt your boss will refuse.

- *Cover for your boss in a crisis.*   Let's assume your boss is away on an important business trip when a crisis suddenly erupts at work requiring quick decisions. She can't even be reached by phone. You have two choices: either call in a senior manager or make the decisions yourself. If you call a senior manager, your boss will suddenly look bad. But if you're confident you can take over, I urge you to take this course of action. *Warning:* Needless to say, a bad decision will make everyone—you, your boss, and your entire department—look bad. The good news is heroes are born in crisis situations.

- *Take grunt work off your boss's hands.*   When possible, take on grunt work so the boss can concentrate on managerial responsibilities. I don't suggest making this a steady practice. During busy times, even bosses have to do their share of grunt work. But if the opportunity arises, offering to take on some grunt work will allow the boss to concentrate on more critical departmental affairs.

- *Be your boss's advocate should corporate politics get nasty.* Regardless of the company's size, corporate politics are unavoidable. Politics and in-fighting can get especially nasty when there is corporate upheaval. This is when the power players step forward to stake their claim. You might find that your boss is in the middle of a palace revolt, for example. There has been a takeover, and the new regime may want to fire your boss and give the job to their own person. You have the luxury of playing it safe and staying out of the fray. But if you've got guts and are willing to put your own job on the line, stick by your boss and help him through the difficult period. If things should turn bad and he's terminated, there is a good chance he'll take you with him wherever he goes.

There will also be occasions where you'll have an opportunity to defend your boss. For example, it's not uncommon to attend a meeting where your boss is the scapegoat. George Fuller, author of *The Workplace Survival Guide*, says that situations like these dictate you defend your boss. It's especially important if a hostile senior manager is rallying the department against him. It doesn't mean getting nasty or testy. Instead, a quiet and assured defense is recommended. When your boss is wrongly accused, you might calmly say, "I find it hard to believe that Molly would do something like that. That's not her style. She's too conscientious and precise. I should know. I've been working with her for 8 years." Well-placed comments like that usually silence dissenters. Fuller suggests adding, "Why don't I go and ask her right now? I think she ought to have the opportunity to defend herself." That usually ends the discussion.

- *Support your boss through good and bad times.* It's nice knowing you have someone in your corner who supports you. If you were a boss, I'm sure you would appreciate having this person on your side in good and bad times. It's safe to assume that as long as your boss holds his job, your job will be secure. Any boss would consider this kind of worker a priceless gift in the cutthroat corporate world.

KEEP YOUR BOSS INFORMED

Lastly, making your boss look good also involves keeping him or her informed at all times. Advises Fuller, "Always communicate openly with your boss so that he or she isn't blindsided by not being informed about something." Beyond warning her of potential problems, let her know about accomplishments, news, or anything that makes her department look good to the folks in the corner office.

Ideally, if you respect your boss, making her look good could actually be a labor of love. There's a concept you never considered. Many people start out trying to ingratiate themselves with a difficult boss and actually wind up respecting this person.

The moral to the story is to keep an open mind. I wouldn't dare suggest it's possible to actually like all crazy bosses. They could lock me up for a comment like that. But it is possible to understand them so you can at least enjoy a civil and productive working relationship. Only under the best of circumstances can you expect honest and productive communication between you and your boss. Believe it or not, it is achievable. After all, we're talking about human chemistry where logic doesn't always overrule. *Remember:* Every relationship is unique.

Good luck. And no matter how bad things get, leave your weapons at home.

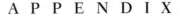
ONE HUNDRED YEARS OF ABUSE

"I CAN'T TAKE IT ANYMORE!"

A SHORT HISTORY OF BAD BOSS BEHAVIOR

We've hurdled from the mechanized industrial era to the supersonic computer age. Along the way, working conditions have improved. So stop bellyaching.

You think you have it bad because your boss is all over you and doesn't give you a moment's peace. You say he's your worst nightmare. He's the reason for your divorce, not to mention your addiction to alcohol, drugs, and food. He's also responsible for your children dropping out of school and joining a mystical cult, not to mention your rejection of your supportive mother who fed, clothed, and loved you more than life itself. Your boss is single-handedly responsible for ruining your life, and you've had it!

It sounds terrible, but if it's any consolation to you, this horror story isn't all that bad. There is no question the mythical worker just described is experiencing hard times. But it could be worse. His boss could have had him seriously hurt, permanently disfigured, or killed.

History provides some powerful lessons you need to consider before you visit a new therapist or take out a contract on your boss's life. If you think your boss is a nut case, consider what your ancestors had to put up with over a century ago.

That's before the labor and human rights movements, the Equal Employment Opportunity Commission, diversity awareness, and all that humane stuff that led to the creation of the "feeling, worker-centered boss."

Robert Zieger, a labor movement expert and professor of history at the University of Florida in Gainesville, reminds us that historically there has always been tension between workers and bosses. "It's a relationship based upon power," he explains.

Zieger reminds us that hardly a century ago a serious disagreement with your boss could lead to having both your legs broken—or even something worse. In the early 1900s, workers were at the mercy of their bosses. Few rules protected them from what was known as the "Drive System." American industry was reaping the benefits of industrialization and mass production and didn't much care about workers' rights and grievances. This was the era when legendary straw bosses dominated assembly lines across America with an iron fist. They were tough, ruthless, and didn't care what their workers thought of them.

The straw boss was an empire unto himself. On assembly-line floors, he was as close to a god as you could get. Physical confrontations between bosses and employees were common. Naturally, employees usually came up short. Even if they had the satisfaction of decking their boss, they wound up on the unemployment line, which was a far worse fate.

During World War I, new boss-worker patterns began to emerge as many large employers assumed a paternalistic attitude toward their workers. Whether they sincerely wanted to improve working conditions or simply deemed it good public relations, these token gestures hinted that change was in the wind.

Automobile pioneer Henry Ford is credited with improving worker conditions by introducing the $5 day in 1914. A brilliant entrepreneur, Ford knew the power of the almighty dollar. But he also knew how to win worker loyalty and curry public favor. By the same token, he had no intention of giving anything away. By guaranteeing workers $5 a day, he increased productivity, reduced turnover, and upgraded his reputation by projecting the image of a pioneering boss.

Other employers followed Ford's lead. It didn't take a college education to see the wisdom of his acts. Treat workers decently, pay them a living wage, and you'll get more out of them.

Yet, Ford's widely publicized $5-a-day wage was hard won. This profit-obsessed entrepreneur expected workers to earn their wages. His workers put in grueling hours to get their $5. When they griped and threatened to join a union, Ford showed his true colors. His supervisors, all of whom were ex-convicts and boxers, used brute force to convince workers otherwise. They made it quite clear that there would be no strikes at a Ford plant. Insubordination of any kind would not be tolerated. It would be a cold day in hell before the assembly line would grind to a halt.

Despite Ford's gestures of emancipation, he was a tough and brutal boss who felt that muscle and intimidation were the only ways to keep workers in line. As for his employees, the only thing that got them up at the crack of dawn to report to work was a paycheck at the end of the week. It certainly wasn't the satisfaction that comes from doing a decent day's work. A veteran factory worker who had spent 40 years on Ford's assembly lines neatly summed up what it was like working for the legendary entrepreneur: "It was like working in hell."

By the early 1920s, the concept of welfare capitalism was bandied about by politicians and a few liberal-minded employers running large companies. Intellectuals, workplace scholars, and radicals insisted that workers were more than cogs in wheels and argued for essential amenities such as medical care, stock purchase options, and subsidized housing. Many large organizations, notably telephone and electric companies, began offering essential extras that went beyond the standard paycheck.

But virtually all attempts at improving workers' plights were shattered when the Great Depression brought the

United States to its knees in the early 1930s. Once again it was survival of the fittest. As thousands of companies were catapulted into bankruptcy, all attempts at humane and ethical treatment of employees were abandoned. The American worker was once again the victim of exploitation as companies struggled to survive. If you were lucky enough to find a job, you took whatever was dished out to you. The painful alternative was starvation.

By the end of the Depression, unions were coming into their own and fighting for workers' rights. Franklin Delano Roosevelt's New Deal administration promised a better lot for the backbone of the economy—the American worker. Roosevelt scored big points with American factory workers by promising to improve conditions and to right the differences between management and labor. A worker was quoted in a national newspaper saying, "Roosevelt is the only person who understands that my boss is a son of a bitch."

But idealistic workers who had joined unions thinking they were the panacea to their problems discovered a sea of difference between the promise and the reality of improved conditions. Throughout America, corporate towns were in turmoil as workers and management clashed in bloody confrontations. But the unions were powerful and wouldn't back off until the battle was won and working conditions improved. They demanded better treatment on shop floors, abandonment of the seniority system, and abolition of random layoffs without warning or provocation.

Despite union power and clout, workers quickly discovered that better working conditions don't come easy. In many "rust belt" plants, unions waged long, bloody battles before changes were instituted. There were many casualties and deaths along the way.

By the early 1940s, organized labor was well entrenched, and working conditions had improved dramatically. Companies established a separate department called "employee relations" to create stable coexistent relationships between workers and supervisors. Personnel departments, the forerunners of the modern-day human resources departments, were created to hire and fire workers with diplomacy and to apply fair and unbiased hiring standards.

When the 1950s rolled into place, both labor and management had built fortresslike bureaucracies to protect themselves from each other. Labor had grievance committees at their disposal to settle disputes, and management instituted pseudoscientific controls to monitor performance.

From the 1960s to the present, labor-management relations have continued to change. Over the last 30 years, unions have lost a good deal of clout, and only in the last 5 years have they made a concentrated effort to boost their ranks and revive their power. But while union power wanes, the improvement of worker relations, in theory at least, has been elevated to a priority goal at enlightened companies throughout the country.

In the 1980s, employers were intent on improving the quality of life for workers by bringing them into the decision-making process through the creation of quality circles. Words like *empowerment* and *diversity* were also bandied about in an effort to bridge the historical rift between employees and bosses. Management insisted that the key to building dedicated and loyal workers, not to mention boosting profits, was to empower staffers so they would be part of the decision-making process. The essence of empowerment says, "Hey, guys, we're all in this game together. Let's work toward the same mission and share the same goals."

And diversity, a controversial buzzword because no one understands what it means, is all about appreciating and understanding people's differences. Since America is made up of a diverse melting-pot work force, we ought to devote more time to understanding the unique differences among employees.

All these new developments certainly sound wonderful. Every time a new buzzword makes its way into the common vocabulary, we think that the past is finally behind us and we've evolved to a more civilized, enlightened plateau. Yes, the past is certainly behind us, but as Zieger points out, the barrier

keeping bosses and employers in a perpetual tug-of-war relationship hasn't been removed and never will be. How can it be
when that barrier is *power*? And despite theories, programs,
and new attitudes, it will always be that way.

The good news is, unlike bosses of the 1920s and 1930s,
today's bosses are less likely to bash in your head with a club if
you disagree with them. Instead, they'll try to bullwhip you
mentally until you have a complete nervous breakdown and
are reduced to a babbling mass incapable of blurting out a
coherent sentence. While that's an exaggeration, don't think
there aren't bosses who've come pretty close to wreaking that
kind of psychological havoc. Despite enlightened times, bad
boss behavior never goes away; it just manifests itself differently.

SURVIVAL STRATEGIES FOR GETTING ON WITH DIFFICULT BOSSES

DANGEROUS BEHAVIORS SIGNALING TROUBLE AHEAD

It's easy to resort to dangerous behavior, especially when you're overworked and emotionally and physically exhausted because your tyrannical, megalomaniacal boss has been riding you unmercifully for months on end. Suddenly—often unconsciously—you find yourself involved in bizarre behaviors, such as:

- Stalking your boss late at night.
- Tapping your boss's phone to find a reason for blackmail.
- Considering attaching a pipe bomb to his or her car or hiring a hitperson.
- Writing your boss's spouse to report an affair with his or her assistant.
- Writing to your boss's boss informing her that your boss has been stealing company property or selling industrial secrets to competitors.

- Imagining taking your boss skydiving with a defective parachute.

Solution: To ward off dangerous behaviors, consider the following job-retention strategies.

AFFIRMATIONS TO PURIFY YOUR MIND TO AVOID EVIL THOUGHTS ABOUT YOUR BOSS

1. I will not allow my boss to get to me.
2. Hating my boss is okay, but acting on it could land me on death row or in a tiny prison cell for the rest of my life. (The mystical message is virulent rage is self-defeating, but controlled loathing is acceptable.)
3. Even though my boss is an obnoxious slob, I forgive him because he is an ignorant, mindless lout.
4. There are more pressing life goals—such as eating and meeting my mortgage payments—than hating my boss.
5. My boss is actually just a troubled lost soul with a good heart. (If you can really make yourself believe this, you deserve sainthood.)
6. Even though my boss acts like an untrustworthy bungling nincompoop, there is good in everyone. (The same goes for this one: Believing this could elevate you to martyr status.)
7. Hating my boss is a waste of precious life energy.
8. I forgive my boss all trespasses, he knows not what he does.
9. I pity my boss because she is a dimwitted jerk trying to pretend she's smart.
10. I love my boss, for he is only mortal like the rest of us. (Yuck!)

RECOMMENDED EXERCISES FOR BOSS-HATERS

The goal is to channel the energy you previously used to hate your boss into constructive, healthy exercises so you don't develop ulcers, back problems, or a host of other somatic and psychological ailments.

EXERCISES FOR THE OFFICE

What do you do when your boss is driving you up the wall? Close your office door and drop to the floor and do 200 push-ups, followed by 400 sit-ups and 5 minutes of deep-breathing exercises. If you're still uptight, repeat this regimen. The bad news is that these exercises can practically kill you. The good news is that if you survive them, you can look forward to gigantic Terminator-like arms, washboard abs, and Olympic-caliber stamina.

SOLITARY EXERCISES

- *Yoga.*   This is great for the bean sprout, carrot-munching crowd. There are plenty of books out there that outline dozens of great yoga exercises. You'd be surprised at how much energy you can expel by bending your body like a pretzel and standing on your head for three straight hours. Do it long enough and you may wind up understanding, or even—perish the thought—liking your boss. If it worked for the Maharishi, it can work for you. *Added benefit*: These exercises are great for limbering up the body. The best part is you can do them anywhere—even in your closet.

- *Long-distance walking.*   This is a great tension reliever. If you've had a bad boss day, why not walk home? So what if it's 5 miles; the longer the better. On weekends you can walk to a neighboring state. For vacations, you can walk cross-country. If things are really bad, take a leave of absence and walk around the United States.

- *Marathon running.* I'll bet you didn't know there are marathon aficionados who actually travel around the country to run in different marathons. Every one of these people has a problem with his or her boss and has taken to the asphalt to work it out.

- *Off-road biking.* It's riskier than traditional biking, but it's also a sport that is becoming enormously popular with Americans hungry for weekend adventure. For hard-core off-road country biking on rugged terrain, excellent biking skills are required. It amounts to a great energy release and escape from the pressure of an overbearing boss.

TEAM SPORTS

If you're a people person, a host of highly recommended tension-relieving sports are perfect for you. I endorse strenuous physical efforts such as racquetball, tennis, volleyball, football, and basketball, all of which require massive energy outputs. The more brutal the sport, the more energy you work off, thus making you more effective at dealing with the vagaries of a crazy boss.

Dangerous Sports to A void. Many hideous bosses have driven employees to dangerous life-threatening sports to reconfirm their self-worth. Even though your boss is a despot, think twice before you put your life on the line and pursue a life-threatening sport. Avoid boxing, sumo-wrestling, mountain-climbing, dog-sledding, hang-gliding, sky-diving, and big-game hunting.

INDEX

ABOUT THE AUTHOR

Bob Weinstein is a nationally known career expert, syndicated columnist, and author of 10 highly acclaimed books, including *Who Says There Are No Jobs Out There?* He lives and works in New York City.